ILLUSTRATED ADVANCED BIOLOGY

Green Plants

the inside story

C J Clegg

JOHN MURRAY

Data and artwork credits

The author would like to thank the following for giving permission to redraw or adapt artwork and data:

Figure 2.2 (p.3) data for part (2) from Monteith, J.L. (1962) *Netherlands Journal of Agricultural Science* 10, 5: 334–346; **Figure 2.6** (p.6) photographs from Whittingham, C.P. (1964) *The Chemistry of Plant Processes*, Methuen, London, facing p.144; **Figure 2.23** (p.17) adapted from Bonner, J. and Galston, A.W. (1958) *Principles of Plant Physiology*, W.H. Freeman & Co., San Francisco; **Figure 2.25** (p.18) adapted from Hewitt, E.J. and Smith, T.A. (1974) *Plant Mineral Nutrition*, Edinburgh University Press, Edinburgh, p.107; **Figure 2.31** (p.22) Gunning, B.E.S. and Pate, J.S. (ed. Robards, A.W.) (1974) *Dynamic Aspects of Plant Ultrastructure*, reproduced with the permission of McGraw-Hill International UK Ltd; **Figure 3.4** (p.25) micrograph courtesy of Greenwood, A.D., in Hall, D.O. and Rao, K.K. (1972) *Photosynthesis*, Studies in Biology no. 37, Edward Arnold (Publishers) Ltd, London, facing p.29; **Figure 4.6** (p.37) adapted from Hubbard, C.E. (1954) *Grasses*, Penguin, Harmondsworth, Middlesex; **Figure 4.10** (p.39) adapted from West, R.G. (1971) *Studying the Past by Pollen Analysis*, Oxford Biology Reader, p.7, figure 8, reprinted by permission of Oxford University Press; **Figure 4.21** (p.45) adapted from Ingrouille, M. (1992) *Diversity and Evolution of Land Plants*, Chapman & Hall, London, p.85, reproduced with the kind permission of Klower Academic Publishers; **Figure 4.27** (p.49) adapted from James, C. (2000) *Global Review of Commercialized Transgenic Crops: 2000*, International Service for the Acquisition of Agri-biotech Applications (ISAAA), Ithaca, New York; **Figure 5.3** (p.50) data from Vaughan, J.G. and Geissler, C.A. (1997) *The New Oxford Book of Food Plants*, Oxford University Press, Oxford; **Figure 5.4** (p.51) from data in Janick, J., Schery, R.W., Woods, F.W. and Ruttan, V.W. (1974) *Plant Sciences – An Introduction to World Crops*, 2nd edn, W.H. Freeman & Co., San Francisco; **Figure 5.9** (p.53) graph adapted from Harper, J.E. *et al.* (1985) *Exploitation of Physiological and Genetic Variability to Enhance Crop Productivity*, American Society of Crop Physiologists, Purdue, Indiana; **Figure 5.10** (p.53) data from MAFF (now DEFRA), Statistics (Census and Surveys) Division. Copyright material is reproduced under Class Licence Number C02P000060 with the permission of the Controller of HMSO; **Figures 5.17 and 5.18** (p.57) adapted from www.mpizkoeln.mpg.de/~pr/garten/schau/Sorghumbicolor/Sorghum.html Max Planck Institute for Plant Breeding Research; **Figure 5.21** (p.58) Azolla plants adapted from Ingrouille, M. (1992) *Diversity and Evolution of Land Plants*, Chapman & Hall, London, p.238, figure 7.6; leaf section adapted from Smith, G.M. (1955) *Cryptogamic Botany II Bryophytes and Pteridophytes*, McGraw Hill, New York/London, p.375, figure 250; graph adapted from Moran, R.C. (1997) 'The little nitrogen factories', *Biological Sciences Review* 10(2): 2–6, p.5; **Table 5.1** (p.60) from Janick, J., Scherry, R.W., Woods, F.W. and Ruttan, V.W. (1974) *Plant Sciences: An Introduction to World Crops*, W.H. Freeman & Co., San Francisco,

pp.435 and 441; **Figure 6.5** (p.66) graph adapted from Villiers, T.A. (1972) 'Seed dormancy', in: *Seed Biology*, Vol. III (Kozlowski, T.T., ed.), Academic Press, New York, pp. 219–281; **Figure 6.6** (p.67) graph adapted from Webb, D.P., van Staden, J. and Wareing, P.F. (1973) *Journal of Experimental Botany* 24: 105; **Figure 6.10** (p.68) graph adapted from Thimann, K.V. (1934) *Journal of General Physiology* 18: 32; **Figure 6.11** (p.69) adapted from Bonner, J. and Walston, A.W. (1958) *Principles of Plant Physiology*, W.H. Freeman & Co., San Francisco, pp. 373–374; **Figure 8.11** (p.87) adapted from Thomas, P. (2000) *Trees: Their Natural History*, Cambridge University Press, Cambridge, p.167, figure 6.3; **Figure A2.1** (p.88) from data in MacDouglas, D.T. (1936) Carnegie Institute, Washington, Publication 462, Washington, DC.

Photo credits

Thanks are due to the following copyright holders for permission to reproduce photographs:

Cover Simon Burt/Apex; **p.2** Gene Cox; **p.5** *all* Gene Cox; **p.8** Gene Cox; **p.9** Gene Cox; **p.10** Gene Cox; **p.11** Gene Cox; **p.12** *all* Gene Cox; **p.13** *all* Gene Cox; **p.21** Science Photo Library/Volker Steger; **p.25** *t* Science Photo Library/Kari Lounatmaa; **p.34** Holt Studios; **p.35** *tl, bl, cl & cr* C.J. Clegg; *br* Natural Visions; **p.36** *l* Natural Visions; *r* Gene Cox; **p.38** *all* Gene Cox; **p.39** Gene Cox; **p.40** Gene Cox; **p.41** *l* C.J. Clegg; *r* Science Photo Library/Jeremy Burgess; **p.42** Gene Cox; **p.43** *all* Gene Cox; **p.46** C.J. Clegg; **p.47** *l* Science Photo Library/Keith Seaman/Agstock; *r* Science Photo Library/Jeremy Burgess; **p.48** *all* C.J. Clegg; **p.49** Science Photo Library/John Mead; **p.51** *l & r* C.J. Clegg; **p.52** Gene Cox; **p.53** *tr & br* C.J. Clegg; *bl* Science Photo Library/Bill Bachman; **p.54** Gene Cox; **p.56** *t* Holt Studios; *b* Gene Cox; **p.59** *t* Natural Visions; *c* Gene Cox; *b* Dr M.B. Jackson, IACR – Long Ashton Research Station, Bristol, UK; **p.60** *t* Natural Visions; *bl & br* Holt Studios; **p.61** *t* Holt Studios; *bl & br* C.J. Clegg; **p.62** *t* Holt Studios; *b* J & P Parker, Paparola, Northland, New Zealand; **p.63** *l & r* Holt Studios; **p.68** *l & r* Gene Cox; **p.71** *l* C.J. Clegg; *r* Science Photo Library/Dana Downie/ Agstock; **p.72** *l* C.J. Clegg; *r* John Townson/ Creation; **p.74** *l & r* C.J. Clegg; **p.76** *l* C.J. Clegg; *r* Gene Cox; **p.77** *t* Natural Visions; *bl & br* C.J. Clegg; **p.78** *t & b* Gene Cox; **p.79** *tl* Holt Studios; *tr* Science Photo Library/Jeremy Burgess; *b* C.J. Clegg; **p.80** *tr, cl & b* C.J. Clegg, *cr* Gene Cox; *br* Holt Studios; **p.81** Gene Cox; **p.82** Gene Cox; **p.83** *t & b* Gene Cox; **p.84** *tl* Holt Studios; *cl, bl & r* Gene Cox; **p.85** Gene Cox; **p.86** *tr & cr* C.J. Clegg; *cl & br* Gene Cox; **p.87** C.J. Clegg.

t = top, *b* = bottom, *l* = left, *r* = right, *c* = centre

Every effort has been made to contact copyright holders but if any have been inadvertently overlooked the Publishers will be pleased to make the necessary arrangements at the earliest opportunity.

Illustrations by Tony Jones/Art Construction
Layouts by Eric Drewery
Cover design by John Townson/Creation

Typeset in 10/12pt Galliard by Wearset Ltd, Boldon, Tyne and Wear
Printed and bound in Spain by Bookprint, S.L., Barcelona

A catalogue entry for this title is available from the British Library

ISBN 0 7195 7553 2

Contents

Abbreviations used in Figure captions and labels

TS	= transverse section		HP	= high power (magnification)
LS	= longitudinal section		LP	= low power
RLS	= radial longitudinal section		SEM	= scanning electron micrograph
TLS	= tangential longitudinal section		TEM	= transmission electron micrograph

Preface

Green plants make everything possible! Animals rely on plants for their food, either directly (herbivores) or indirectly (carnivores). The essential conditions of the biosphere are dependent on the working plant – without photosynthesis, atmospheric oxygen levels could not be maintained, and by it the levels of the 'greenhouse gas' carbon dioxide are kept low, on a daily basis. In their turn, green plants are dependent on microorganisms of decay to recycle all the inorganic nutrients used in photosynthesis.

Humans exploit plants in every way imaginable. We need them for food, fuel, clothing, drugs and medicines, and numerous industrial, scientific and technical applications. Vast numbers of plants are grown for decorative display – the cultivation of plants is a major leisure pursuit. The Eden Project's conservatories, built in giant craters in the Cornish landscape, have become the eighth wonder of the world! Millions of people visit conservation projects like this, and parks and garden, botanic gardens and nature reserves in full flower, with obvious enthusiasm.

Consequently, we should not be ignorant of plants (and none should suggest they are boring!), for the study of plant life is fundamental to understanding the living world. This book tackles issues of the working plant in an illustrated way, using photographs, photomicrographs, line drawings and flow diagrams, as well as concise text.

Related publications

In the same series, published by John Murray:

Clegg, C.J. (1998) *Mammals: Structure & Function* 0 7195 7551 6
Clegg, C.J. (1999) *Genetics & Evolution* 0 7195 7552 4
Clegg, C.J. (2002) *Microbes in Action* 0 7195 7554 0

Taking your studies further

- Royal Botanical Gardens at Kew: www.rbgkew.org.uk
- Royal Botanic Garden Edinburgh: www.rbge.org.uk
- Eden Project: www.edenproject.com
- The Linnean Society of London: www.linnean.org
- Science and Plants for Schools: www-saps.plantsci.cam.ac.uk
- Royal Horticultural Society: www.rhs.org.uk
- New Scientist: www.newscientist.com
- University botanic gardens, including: www.chelseaphysicgarden.co.uk
                                      www.ashmol.ox.ac.uk/omc/oxmus242.html

Acknowledgements

To all the researchers, teachers, illustrators and writers who have influenced my own understanding I gladly acknowledge my debt. Where copyright material has been used it is detailed on page ii. If the intellectual property of anyone has been used without prior agreement then I ask that John Murray (Publishers) Ltd are contacted so that correction can be made.

I have benefited from specific advice and comments from: Dr Richard D. Firn, University of York; Dr Claire Halpin, University of Dundee; Dr Jim M. Dunwell, University of Reading; Dr Richard P.C. Johnson, formerly of University of Aberdeen; and Dr Erica Clark of the Science and Plants for Schools Project, University of Cambridge. Nevertheless, any remaining errors are my responsibility.

I am indebted to Katie Mackenzie Stuart, Amy Austin and Helen Townson at John Murray, and to Gina Walker, Science Editor, whose skill and patience have brought together text and illustrations as I have wished.

Dr Chris Clegg
Salisbury, Wiltshire, 2003

Green plants – the variety

The green plants make up one of the five Kingdoms of living things (Figure 1.1). Green plants include the **mosses** and liverworts, the clubmosses and horsetails, the **ferns**, the **conifers**, and the **flowering plants** (Figure 1.2). In the long history of life, green plants evolved about 500 million years ago from aquatic, single-celled organisms called green algae (possibly very similar to *Chlorella* – page 33).

A green plant is an organism with:

- a wall around each cell whose chief component is **cellulose** – cellulose is a polysaccharide and is an extremely tough, protective material
- cell organelles called **chloroplasts**, the site of photosynthesis – by photosynthesis the plant generates energy-rich nutrients from simple, inorganic substances (CO_2, H_2O and ions)
- an unusual life cycle, with two distinct stages or **generations that alternate** – one generation produces spores, the other produces gametes (sex cells). The evolutionary significance of this is discussed on page 44.

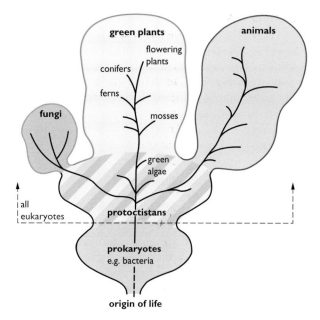

Figure 1.1 The five Kingdoms of living things.

Flowering plants

This book is mainly about flowering plants, particularly the non-woody ones, known as **herbaceous** flowering plants (as opposed to the trees and shrubs). Today the flowering plants are the dominant terrestrial plants. The fossil record indicates that they achieved this dominance early in their evolutionary history – about 100 million years ago. In successfully adapting to terrestrial conditions, flowering plants evolved:

- ground tissues that support stems and leaves in the air
- **xylem** vessels for the internal transport of water
- **phloem** elements for the internal transport of nutrients, e.g. sucrose, amino acids
- mechanisms for reducing water loss from their stems and leaves.

1 Tabulate the differences between prokaryote and eukaryote cells.

2 Ecologists ask 'Have you thanked a green plant today?' Why?

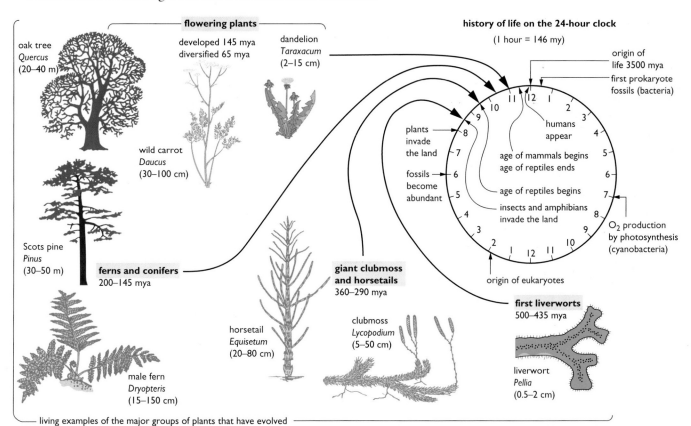

Figure 1.2 The history of life on the 24-hour clock and the diversity of green plants.

The working plant

Mesophyll cells

A key to the success of flowering plants is their **autotrophic** nutrition, involving photosynthesis in the **mesophyll cells** of the leaves of green plants. These cells are one of half a dozen different types found in flowering plants (pages 9–13). Mesophyll cells (Figure 2.1) contain **chloroplasts** (page 25), the organelles where photosynthesis occurs. Typically, 50–100 chloroplasts are present in a mesophyll cell, making up about 90% of the volume of the **cytoplasm**.

I How does heterotrophic nutrition of animals differ from plant nutrition?

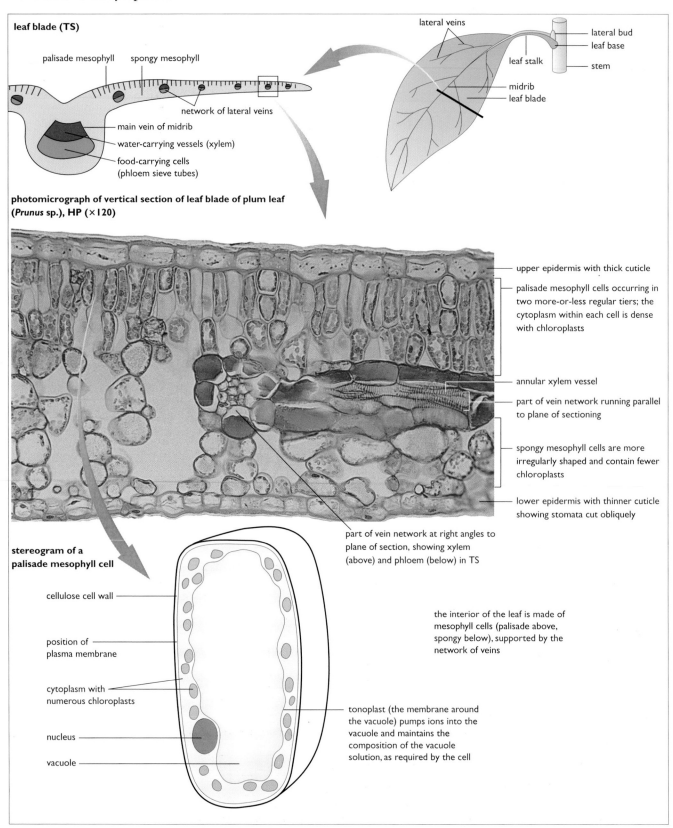

leaf blade (TS)

palisade mesophyll   spongy mesophyll

network of lateral veins

main vein of midrib

water-carrying vessels (xylem)

food-carrying cells (phloem sieve tubes)

lateral veins

lateral bud
leaf base

stem

leaf stalk

midrib
leaf blade

photomicrograph of vertical section of leaf blade of plum leaf (*Prunus* sp.), HP (×120)

upper epidermis with thick cuticle

palisade mesophyll cells occurring in two more-or-less regular tiers; the cytoplasm within each cell is dense with chloroplasts

annular xylem vessel

part of vein network running parallel to plane of sectioning

spongy mesophyll cells are more irregularly shaped and contain fewer chloroplasts

lower epidermis with thinner cuticle showing stomata cut obliquely

part of vein network at right angles to plane of section, showing xylem (above) and phloem (below) in TS

stereogram of a palisade mesophyll cell

cellulose cell wall

position of plasma membrane

cytoplasm with numerous chloroplasts

nucleus

vacuole

the interior of the leaf is made of mesophyll cells (palisade above, spongy below), supported by the network of veins

tonoplast (the membrane around the vacuole) pumps ions into the vacuole and maintains the composition of the vacuole solution, as required by the cell

Figure 2.1 The location and structure of mesophyll cells.

What photosynthesis entails

By photosynthesis, glucose is manufactured in the green plant cell at the expense of carbon dioxide absorbed from the air (Figure 2.2). Some of this glucose is respired to provide energy. Some provides the carbon skeletons from which all other biochemicals required by the plant are synthesised. Typically, excess glucose is stored as starch.

Figure 2.2 What photosynthesis entails.

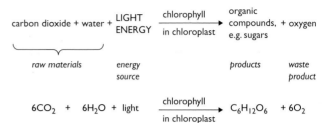

1 photosynthesis in summary

carbon dioxide + water + LIGHT ENERGY $\xrightarrow[\text{in chloroplast}]{\text{chlorophyll}}$ organic compounds, + oxygen e.g. sugars

raw materials　　　energy source　　　products　　waste product

$$6CO_2 + 6H_2O + \text{light} \xrightarrow[\text{in chloroplast}]{\text{chlorophyll}} C_6H_{12}O_6 + 6O_2$$

Only in the light do leaves take in carbon dioxide (in the dark they are net exporters of CO_2). However, globally, photosynthesis in the light is on such a huge scale as to remove all (or almost all) CO_2 given out by respiration of animals, plants and all microorganisms, and by our combustion of fossil fuels, throughout the 24 hour period (see Figure 3.1, page 24).

2 photosynthesis and the atmosphere

a study of the variation in the concentration of carbon dioxide in the air between the leaves of a green plant – in darkness and during the daylight

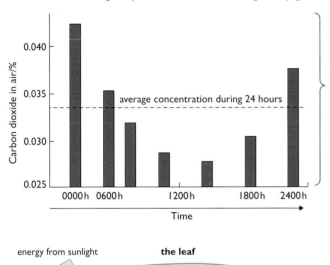

3 photosynthesis in plant nutrition

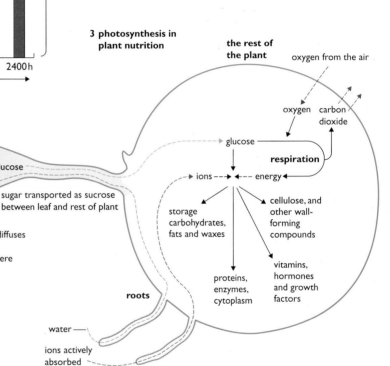

The leaf as a factory for photosynthesis

The green leaf is an organ specialised for photosynthesis. The chief adaptations of the green leaf are identified in Table 2.1.

Table 2.1 Functional adaptations of green leaves

Feature	Function/role
Thin structures with a large surface area	Palisade mesophyll cells spread out over a wide area, maximising the amount of light absorbed
Epidermis of leaf, a single layer of tough, transparent cells with a waxy cuticle	Contains and supports the turgid mesophyll cells, protecting them from invasion by some parasites – and from excess water loss; allows passage of light to cells below
Stomata, the pores in the epidermis (pages 4–7)	Site of inward diffusion of carbon dioxide (and of water vapour out)
Chloroplasts in palisade mesophyll cells	Chloroplasts receive maximum illumination
Continuous air spaces in the mesophyll	Aids gaseous exchange by diffusion
Vein network of leaf (continuous with vascular bundles of stem and roots)	Supports leaf tissue as thin, flexible structure: xylem (page 11) in veins delivers water to cells; phloem (page 10) in veins transports sugar produced to storage sites

Photosynthesis and gas exchange

In the light, carbon dioxide is in very low concentration in the mesophyll cells, compared with air outside the leaf (Figure 2.3). This is because of the enzyme **Rubisco**, present in chloroplasts in large quantities, which fixes carbon dioxide. Consequently, more carbon dioxide diffuses down a concentration gradient into the air spaces of the leaf. Here it dissolves in the surface film of water around mesophyll cells. In solution, the gas diffuses into the chloroplasts. A reverse gradient in oxygen gas results in simultaneous diffusion of oxygen into the air from the green plant cells, in the light. At the same time, water evaporates from the film of water that is bathing cells into the air spaces of the leaf. Water vapour then diffuses into the drier air outside the leaf. All these gas molecules pass in and out through the tiny pores in the epidermis, called **stomata**.

2 Mesophyll cells contain chloroplasts. What other organelles may be present?

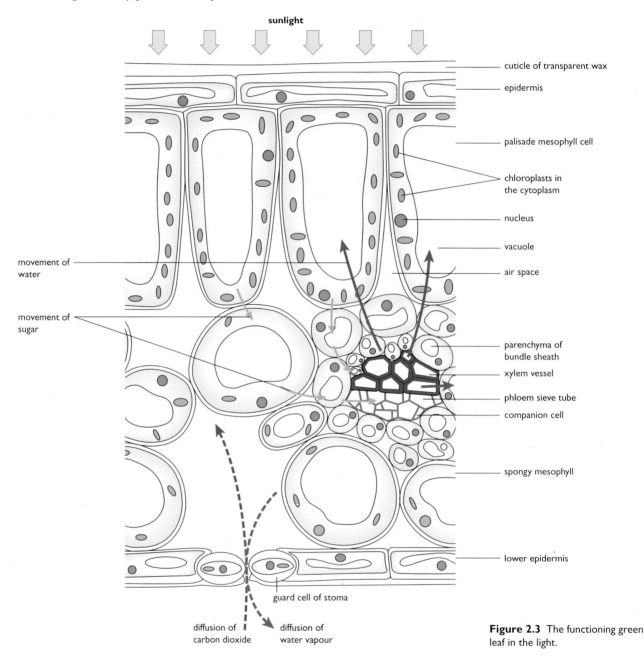

Figure 2.3 The functioning green leaf in the light.

Structure and distribution of stomata

Stomata mostly occur in the epidermis of leaves (some do occur in stems). Each stoma consists of two elongated **guard cells**. These cells are attached to ordinary epidermal cells and securely joined together at each end, but are detached and free to separate along their length, forming a pore between them (Figure 2.4). In the broad, flattened leaf typical of many dicotyledonous plants (page 36), stomata are typically concentrated on the lower epidermis. In the narrow, pointed leaf typical of many monocotyledonous plants, stomata may occur on both surfaces (Figure 2.5).

Figure 2.4 The structure of stomata.

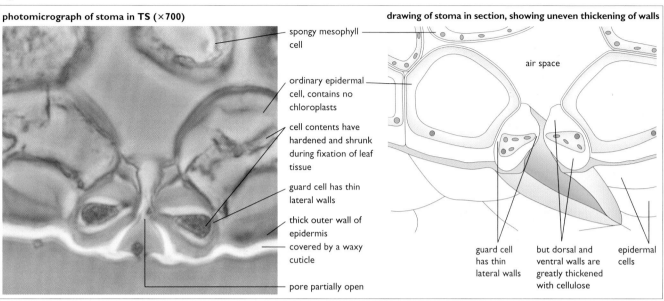

photomicrograph of stoma in TS (×700)

drawing of stoma in section, showing uneven thickening of walls

Figure 2.5 The distribution of stomata.

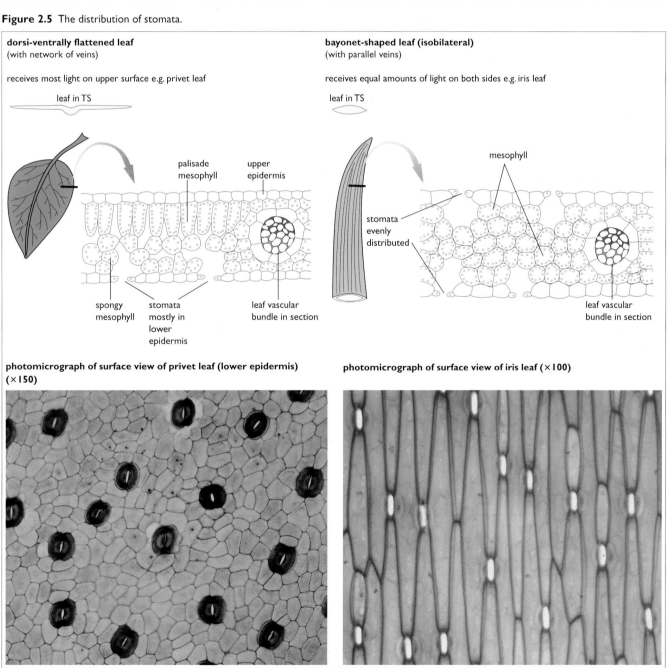

The opening and closing of stomata

Stomata work by turgor pressure (Figure 2.6), opening when water is absorbed by the guard cells from the surrounding epidermal cells. Fully turgid guard cells push into the epidermal cell beside them (because of the way cellulose is laid down in the walls – Figure 2.4, page 5), and a pore develops between the guard cells. When water is lost and the guard cells become flaccid, the pore closes.

Figure 2.6 It's turgor pressure that does it!

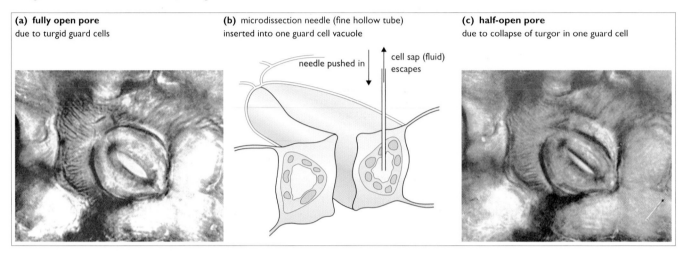

(a) **fully open pore**
due to turgid guard cells

(b) microdissection needle (fine hollow tube) inserted into one guard cell vacuole

needle pushed in

cell sap (fluid) escapes

(c) **half-open pore**
due to collapse of turgor in one guard cell

Opening and closing processes

Stomata tend to open in daylight and be closed in the dark (but there are exceptions to this rule). How are opening and closing co-ordinated with the environment?

    The guard cells contain chloroplasts, but opening is *not* simply due to the slow build-up of sugar by photosynthesis in these chloroplasts, leading to turgor pressure and opening. Opening is a much quicker process. It follows on two biochemical changes:

3 What is 'water potential'?

- potassium ions (K^+, a cation) are pumped into the guard cell vacuole from surrounding cells, by proteins of the plasma membranes (triggered by blue light wavelengths), and by cytokinins (page 65)
- starch, stored in the guard cells, is converted to organic acids, particularly malate – these anions accompany the K^+ cations into the guard cell vacuole.

The accumulation of these substances in the guard cell vacuole is triggered in the light, and causes the water potential there to become more negative. So net uptake of water from the surrounding ordinary epidermal cells occurs, making the guard cells turgid (Figure 2.7).

    Closing is brought about by the reversal of these steps in the dark, or when triggered by the stress hormone abscisic acid (ABA, page 65), produced in leaf cells during wilting.

Figure 2.7 How opening and closing occur.

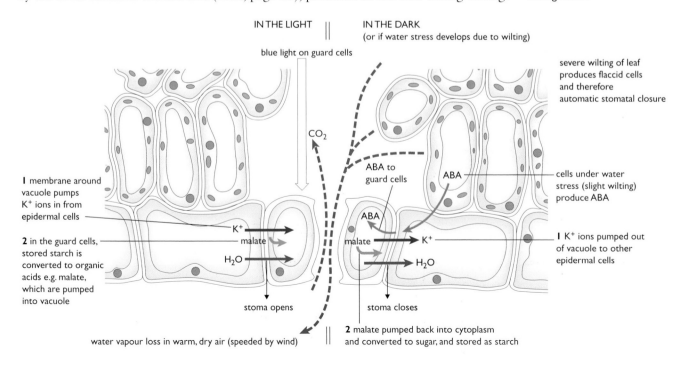

IN THE LIGHT || IN THE DARK
(or if water stress develops due to wilting)

blue light on guard cells

severe wilting of leaf produces flaccid cells and therefore automatic stomatal closure

CO_2

ABA to guard cells

ABA

cells under water stress (slight wilting) produce ABA

1 membrane around vacuole pumps K^+ ions in from epidermal cells

ABA

2 in the guard cells, stored starch is converted to organic acids e.g. malate, which are pumped into vacuole

K^+
malate

malate

K^+

1 K^+ ions pumped out of vacuole to other epidermal cells

H_2O

H_2O

stoma opens

stoma closes

water vapour loss in warm, dry air (speeded by wind)

2 malate pumped back into cytoplasm and converted to sugar, and stored as starch

Extension: the efficiency of stomatal gas exchange

Open stomata occupy only 1–2% of the leaf surface area, yet they permit more than 50% of the diffusion that would occur if the epidermis was entirely absent. This is because:

*   diffusion through small pores is proportional to the perimeter of the pore, not its area – stomatal pores are not round but elliptical, each having a relatively large perimeter
*   if there are very many pores present in the epidermis, diffusion of gases through them is very slow due to interaction of diffusing molecules in overlapping diffusion shells (Figure 2.8).

Figure 2.8 Pores and the diffusion of gases.

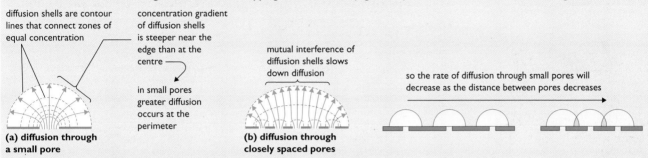

diffusion shells are contour lines that connect zones of equal concentration

concentration gradient of diffusion shells is steeper near the edge than at the centre

in small pores greater diffusion occurs at the perimeter

(a) diffusion through a small pore

mutual interference of diffusion shells slows down diffusion

(b) diffusion through closely spaced pores

so the rate of diffusion through small pores will decrease as the distance between pores decreases

On the other hand, when stomatal pores close (as in a wilted leaf) there is virtually no gas exchange through the epidermis, as the epidermal cells are impervious due to the waxy cuticle. This means there is no further loss of water vapour from the leaf.

Investigating stomatal opening

Can we find out how stomatal apertures change with time of day, changing light intensity, or temperature, for example? Possible ways of doing this are referred to in Figure 2.9.

Figure 2.9 Investigating stomatal aperture.

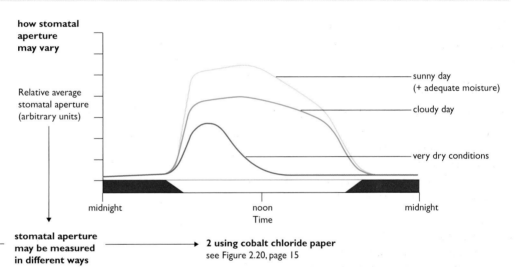

how stomatal aperture may vary

Relative average stomatal aperture (arbitrary units)

sunny day (+ adequate moisture)

cloudy day

very dry conditions

midnight — noon — midnight

Time

stomatal aperture may be measured in different ways

→ **2 using cobalt chloride paper**
see Figure 2.20, page 15

1 using a porometer

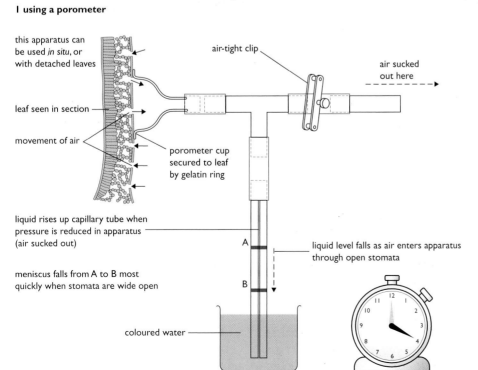

this apparatus can be used *in situ*, or with detached leaves

air-tight clip

air sucked out here

leaf seen in section

movement of air

porometer cup secured to leaf by gelatin ring

liquid rises up capillary tube when pressure is reduced in apparatus (air sucked out)

A

liquid level falls as air enters apparatus through open stomata

meniscus falls from A to B most quickly when stomata are wide open

B

coloured water

Supporting the leaf – the architecture of the plant

The **stem** supports the leaves (Figure 2.10), and transports organic nutrients (amino acids, sugars, etc.) and water and ions between the roots and the whole **aerial system** (leaves, flowers and buds).

The **root system** grows in the soil and provides anchorage for the aerial system. Uptake of water and ions occurs in the root system, and the continuing growth of roots results in new areas of soil being contacted for these resources. Starch storage occurs in root and stem cells.

4 How can you demonstrate that it is the turgidity of cells that supports a herbaceous stem?

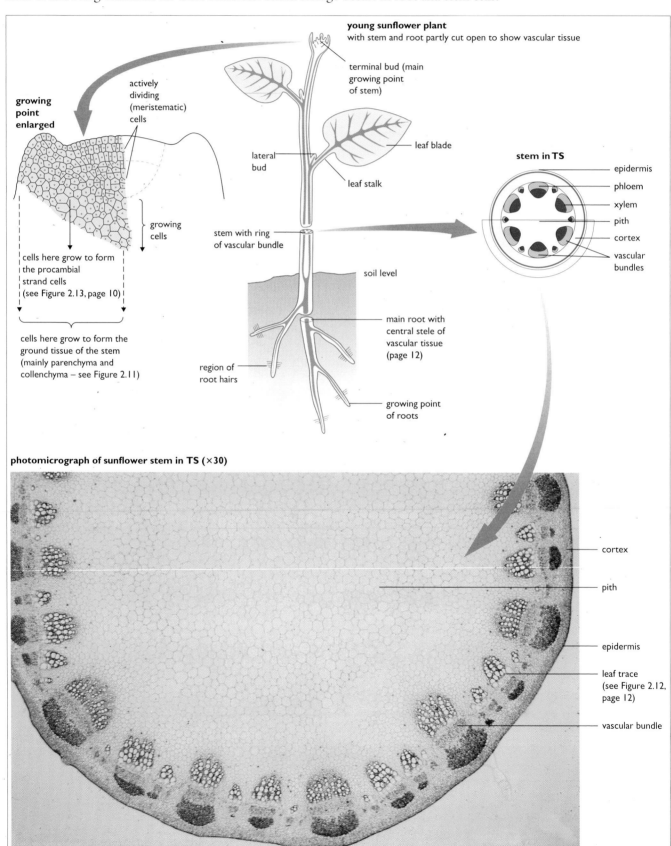

growing point enlarged

actively dividing (meristematic) cells

growing cells

cells here grow to form the procambial strand cells (see Figure 2.13, page 10)

cells here grow to form the ground tissue of the stem (mainly parenchyma and collenchyma – see Figure 2.11)

young sunflower plant with stem and root partly cut open to show vascular tissue

terminal bud (main growing point of stem)

leaf blade

lateral bud

leaf stalk

stem with ring of vascular bundle

soil level

main root with central stele of vascular tissue (page 12)

region of root hairs

growing point of roots

stem in TS

epidermis
phloem
xylem
pith
cortex
vascular bundles

photomicrograph of sunflower stem in TS (×30)

cortex
pith
epidermis
leaf trace (see Figure 2.12, page 12)
vascular bundle

Figure 2.10 The architecture of the plant.

The stem – ground tissues

The ground tissues of **collenchyma** and **parenchyma** (together with some **fibres**) make up the bulk of stem (and root) of herbaceous (non-woody) plants (Figure 2.11). Collenchyma and parenchyma tissues show relatively few structural adaptations. They are concerned with support due to the turgidity of all the living cells contained in the stem. Starch storage also occurs here.

The outermost layer of the stems (and leaves) of herbaceous plants is a continuous layer of compact, tough cells, one cell thick, called **epidermis**. These cells have a layer of wax deposited on the external walls, and their strength and continuity provide mechanical support by counteracting the internal pressure due to turgidity. **Fibres** are different. Here there are no living contents, but their thickened walls are impregnated with lignin, and are extremely tough.

Figure 2.11 The structure of parenchyma, collenchyma and fibres.

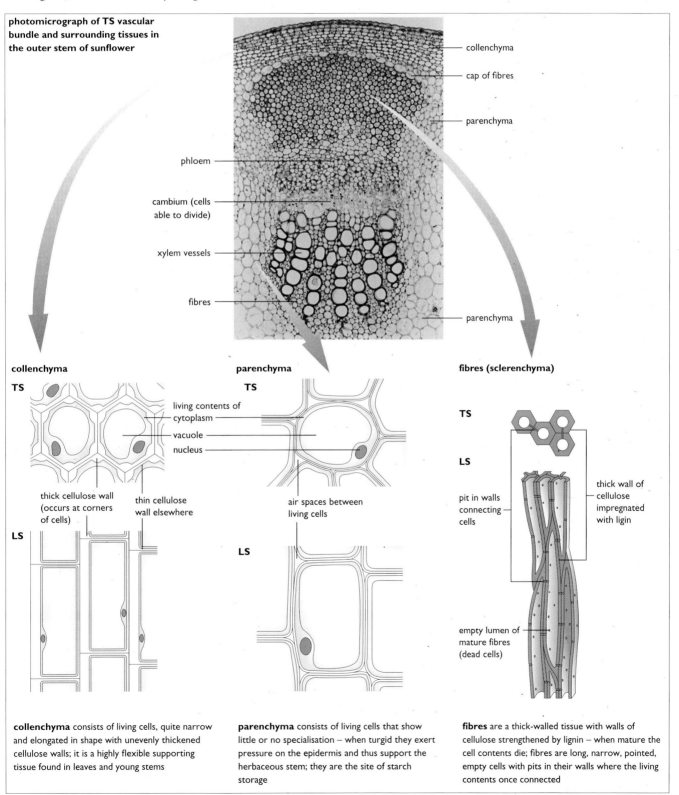

collenchyma consists of living cells, quite narrow and elongated in shape with unevenly thickened cellulose walls; it is a highly flexible supporting tissue found in leaves and young stems

parenchyma consists of living cells that show little or no specialisation – when turgid they exert pressure on the epidermis and thus support the herbaceous stem; they are the site of starch storage

fibres are a thick-walled tissue with walls of cellulose strengthened by lignin – when mature the cell contents die; fibres are long, narrow, pointed, empty cells with pits in their walls where the living contents once connected

The stem – vascular bundles and leaf traces

The vascular bundles of the stem occur in a ring, just below the epidermis. To the outside of this ring is the **cortex** of parenchyma or collenchyma (Figure 2.11, page 9). Within the ring is the **pith**, normally consisting of parenchyma. Large, older stems may be hollow.

This is the arrangement of tissues typical of stems of broad-leaved (dicotyledonous) plants (Figure 2.12). Large vascular bundles alternate with small bundles. The latter are leaf-traces – branches from main bundles that supply leaves attached higher up the stem.

Formation of phloem

At the tip of the stem, just below the terminal bud, vascular tissue (phloem and xylem) is formed from cells of the **procambial strand**. These cells are long and thin compared to surrounding cells of the growing point. Those on the outside of the strand form phloem, those on the inside, xylem.

Mature phloem tissue, the food-transporting tissue, consists of **sieve tubes** and **companion cells**. Sieve tubes lose their nucleus in development and their end walls become perforated by a battery of small holes, forming the **sieve plate.** The companion cells retain a nucleus and have cytoplasmic connections with the contents of the sieve tubes.

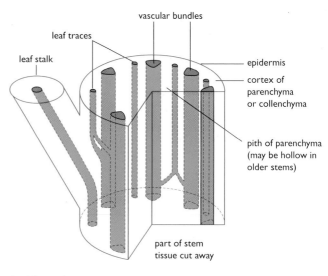

Figure 2.12 The branching vascular system of the dicotyledonous stem.

Figure 2.13 Phloem, formation and structure (TS and LS).

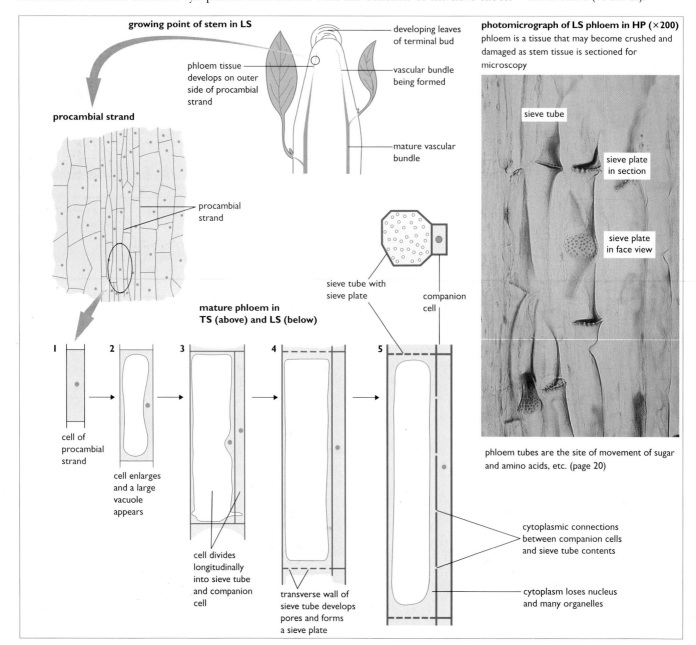

Xylem structure

Xylem vessels are long, hollow tubes in which water travels up the plant. Mature xylem vessels have no living contents, and their end walls have broken down. The lateral walls have additional cellulose layers, added as rings or spiral thickenings in the first-formed xylem (**annular** or **spiral vessels**), or as massive plates of cellulose in the later-formed xylem (**reticular** or **pitted xylem**). These thickenings are impregnated with **lignin**, a chemical, which greatly strengthens them.

5 What chemical stains might you use to show the presence of lignin in thin sections of stem?

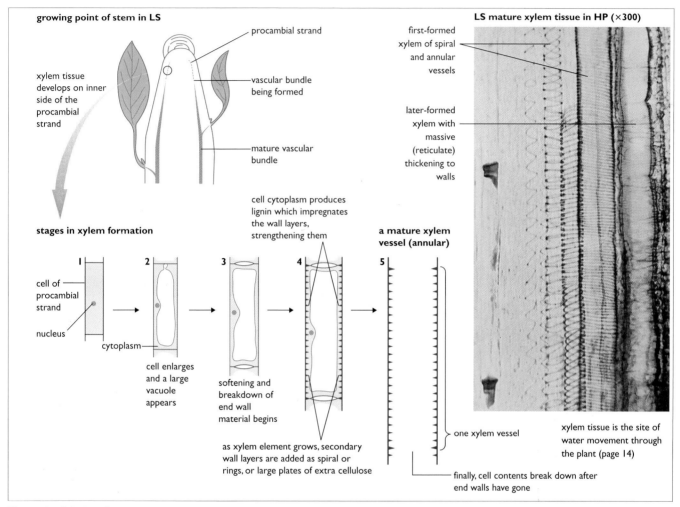

Figure 2.14 Xylem, formation and structure (LS).

Extension: vascular bundles and support of the stem

Stems support the whole aerial system of the plant (leaves, lateral stems, flowers and fruits). The compression forces of this mass of tissue, and the tension and additional compression forces generated by air currents, are resisted. Stems may be compared to a modern ferroconcrete building – with hard, inextensible steel girders (vascular bundles) surrounded by softer, incompressible concrete (turgid parenchyma). The whole stem is held together by the tough epidermis.

Figure 2.15 Stem support.

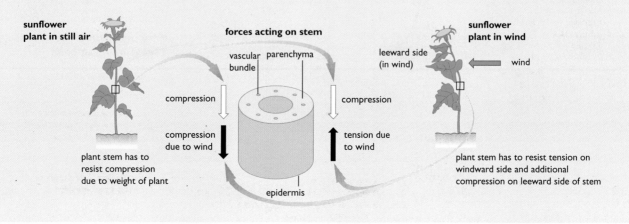

The root – anchorage and absorption

Roots provide anchorage for the aerial system of the plant by branching profusely between the soil particles. A herbaceous plant typically forms 70 kilometres of roots. Either a **tap root system** (Figure 6.9, page 68), typical of broadleaved (dicotyledonous) plants, or a **fibrous root system** (Figure 5.13, page 54), common in the grasses (monocotyledonous plants), is formed. The uptake of water (page 14) and of mineral salts as ions (page 16) is carried out at or near the root tips. The tips of roots grow continuously and come into contact with a huge volume of soil. However, absorption occurs only in the region of **root hairs** (Figure 2.16), behind the growing point of the root tip. It is the root hairs that provide the huge surface area for absorption. Further back along a mature root, the outer surface becomes impervious (Figure 2.17).

6 How do the properties of cellulose make it an ideal plant wall material?

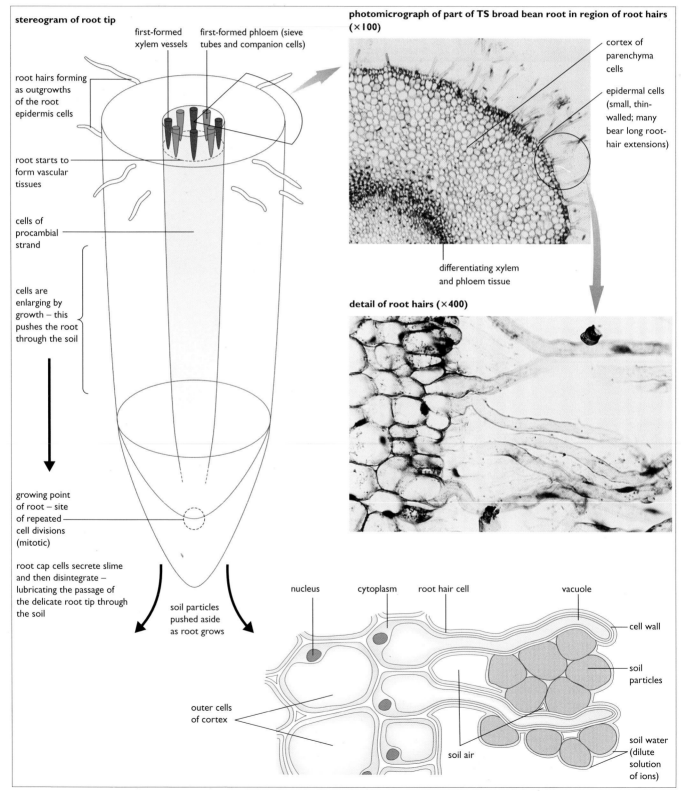

Figure 2.16 The region of root hairs and absorption.

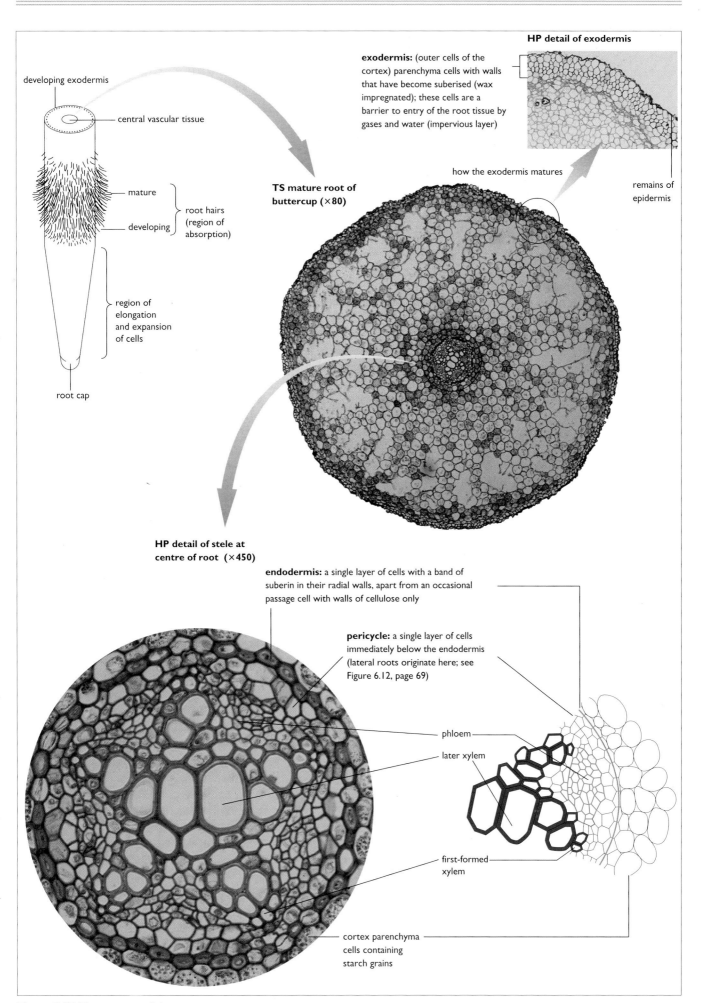

developing exodermis

central vascular tissue

mature
developing
} root hairs (region of absorption)

region of elongation and expansion of cells

root cap

TS mature root of buttercup (×80)

exodermis: (outer cells of the cortex) parenchyma cells with walls that have become suberised (wax impregnated); these cells are a barrier to entry of the root tissue by gases and water (impervious layer)

HP detail of exodermis

how the exodermis matures

remains of epidermis

HP detail of stele at centre of root (×450)

endodermis: a single layer of cells with a band of suberin in their radial walls, apart from an occasional passage cell with walls of cellulose only

pericycle: a single layer of cells immediately below the endodermis (lateral roots originate here; see Figure 6.12, page 69)

phloem

later xylem

first-formed xylem

cortex parenchyma cells containing starch grains

Figure 2.17 The structure of the mature root.

Transport of water through the plant

Water uptake occurs from the soil solution at the root hairs, largely by mass flow through the interconnecting 'free' spaces in the cellulose cell walls (**apoplast** – Figure 2.18). At the **endodermis**, a waxy strip in the radial walls blocks the passage of water by this route momentarily, and water passes by osmosis. Meanwhile, in the leaves evaporation of water occurs and water vapour diffuses out of the stomata (**transpiration**). Water lost by leaf cells is replaced by water from the xylem vessels of the network of veins there. Consequently, a stream of water is drawn up the xylem of the stem by a force generated by transpiration in the leaves. A continuous column of water is maintained, moving from root cell walls to leaf cell walls. Much of this water evaporates and is lost from the plant as vapour.

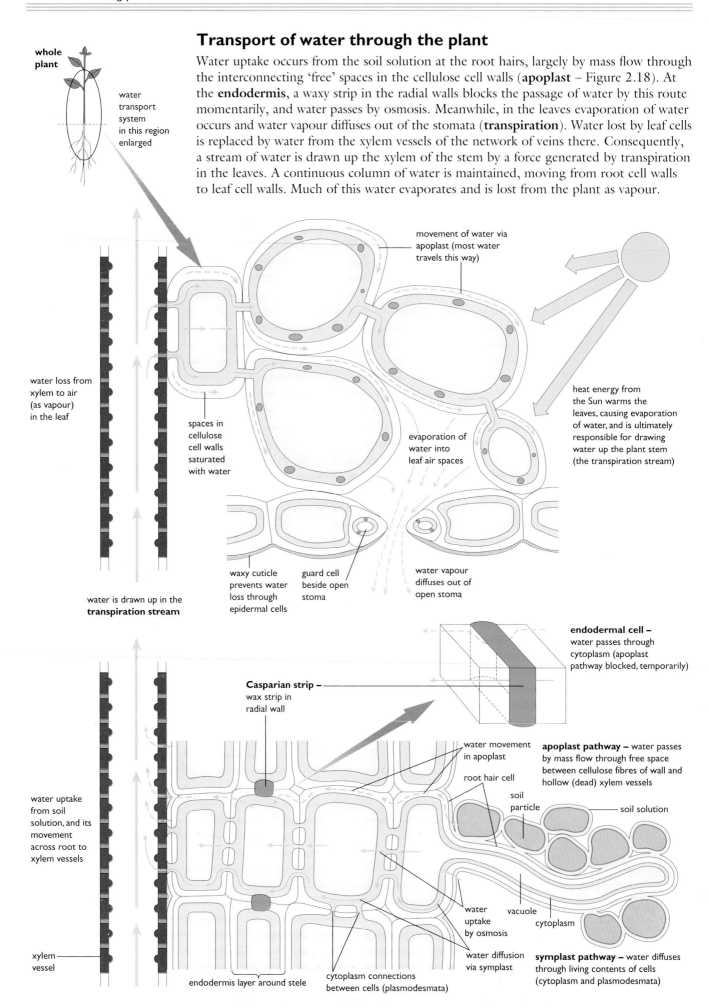

whole plant

water transport system in this region enlarged

movement of water via apoplast (most water travels this way)

heat energy from the Sun warms the leaves, causing evaporation of water, and is ultimately responsible for drawing water up the plant stem (the transpiration stream)

water loss from xylem to air (as vapour) in the leaf

spaces in cellulose cell walls saturated with water

evaporation of water into leaf air spaces

waxy cuticle prevents water loss through epidermal cells

guard cell beside open stoma

water vapour diffuses out of open stoma

water is drawn up in the **transpiration stream**

endodermal cell – water passes through cytoplasm (apoplast pathway blocked, temporarily)

Casparian strip – wax strip in radial wall

water movement in apoplast

root hair cell

apoplast pathway – water passes by mass flow through free space between cellulose fibres of wall and hollow (dead) xylem vessels

soil particle

soil solution

water uptake from soil solution, and its movement across root to xylem vessels

water uptake by osmosis

vacuole

cytoplasm

xylem vessel

endodermis layer around stele

cytoplasm connections between cells (plasmodesmata)

water diffusion via symplast

symplast pathway – water diffuses through living contents of cells (cytoplasm and plasmodesmata)

Figure 2.18 Water uptake and loss by a green plant.

Measuring transpiration

By means of a **potometer** (Figure 2.19), the conditions that affect transpiration (humidity of the air, temperature and air movements) may be investigated. The potometer measures water uptake by the shoot, and in the potometer the shoot has an unlimited supply of water. By contrast, in the intact plant the supply of water from the roots may slow down (e.g. in drought), so water supply is also a factor in the rate of transpiration. The loss of water vapour from leaves can be investigated using dry cobalt chloride paper (Figure 2.20).

7 How could you show that water travels up the stem in the xylem?

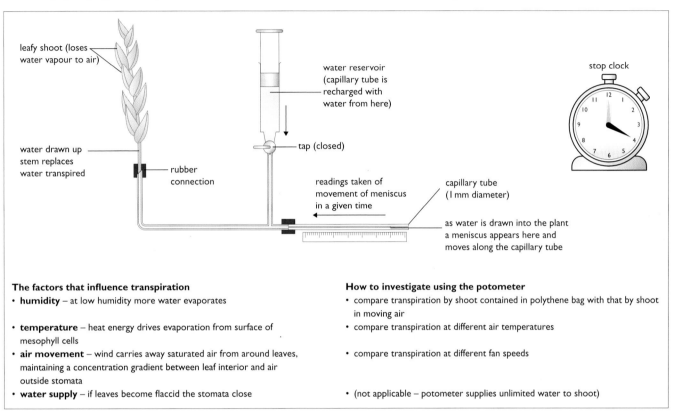

The factors that influence transpiration
- **humidity** – at low humidity more water evaporates

- **temperature** – heat energy drives evaporation from surface of mesophyll cells
- **air movement** – wind carries away saturated air from around leaves, maintaining a concentration gradient between leaf interior and air outside stomata
- **water supply** – if leaves become flaccid the stomata close

How to investigate using the potometer
- compare transpiration by shoot contained in polythene bag with that by shoot in moving air
- compare transpiration at different air temperatures

- compare transpiration at different fan speeds

- (not applicable – potometer supplies unlimited water to shoot)

Figure 2.19 Investigating transpiration using a potometer.

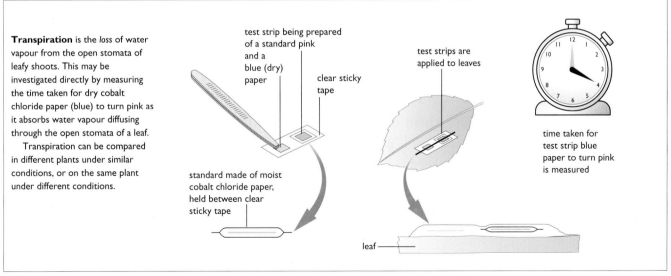

Transpiration is the *loss* of water vapour from the open stomata of leafy shoots. This may be investigated directly by measuring the time taken for dry cobalt chloride paper (blue) to turn pink as it absorbs water vapour diffusing through the open stomata of a leaf.
   Transpiration can be compared in different plants under similar conditions, or on the same plant under different conditions.

Figure 2.20 Comparing water vapour loss from intact plants.

Does transpiration have a role?

Transpiration is a consequence of plant structure, plant nutrition and the mechanism of gaseous exchange in the leaves. In order to manufacture sugars using sunlight energy, water vapour loss from the leaves is inevitable. The plant is, in effect, a 'wick', steadily drying the soil in which it is rooted. However, evaporation has a cooling effect on leaf cells, and the stream of water travelling up the stem carries essential ions from their sites of absorption from the soil to living cells of the aerial system.

Ion uptake by the plant

Terrestrial plants absorb essential ions from the soil solution through their roots. The elements required for plant growth (additional to those supplied in CO_2 and H_2O), and the quantities they are normally required in, were discovered using water culture techniques (Figure 2.21). Some ions are required in relatively large quantities – called **macronutrients** (e.g. nitrate and phosphate ions). Others are required in tiny amounts – the **micronutrients** or **trace elements** (e.g. manganese and iron) (Table 2.2, page 19).

Figure 2.21 Investigating essential ions for plant metabolism.

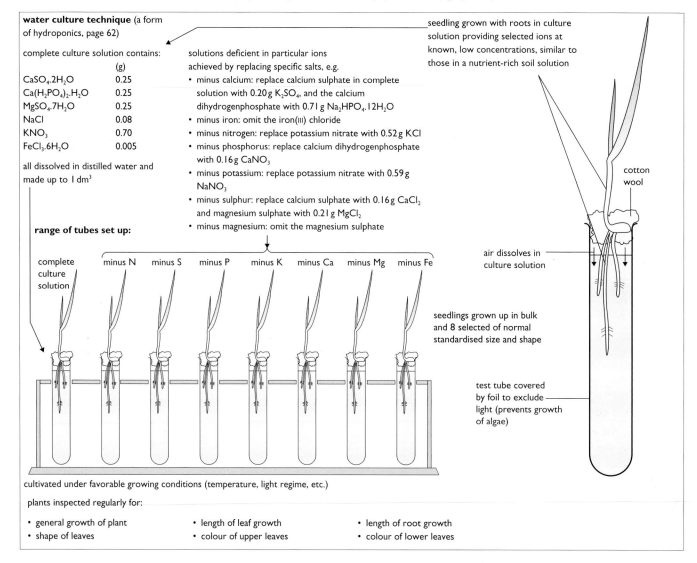

water culture technique (a form of hydroponics, page 62)

complete culture solution contains:

	(g)
$CaSO_4.2H_2O$	0.25
$Ca(H_2PO_4)_2.H_2O$	0.25
$MgSO_4.7H_2O$	0.25
NaCl	0.08
KNO_3	0.70
$FeCl_3.6H_2O$	0.005

all dissolved in distilled water and made up to 1 dm³

solutions deficient in particular ions achieved by replacing specific salts, e.g.
- minus calcium: replace calcium sulphate in complete solution with 0.20 g K_2SO_4, and the calcium dihydrogenphosphate with 0.71 g $Na_2HPO_4.12H_2O$
- minus iron: omit the iron(III) chloride
- minus nitrogen: replace potassium nitrate with 0.52 g KCl
- minus phosphorus: replace calcium dihydrogenphosphate with 0.16 g $CaNO_3$
- minus potassium: replace potassium nitrate with 0.59 g $NaNO_3$
- minus sulphur: replace calcium sulphate with 0.16 g $CaCl_2$ and magnesium sulphate with 0.21 g $MgCl_2$
- minus magnesium: omit the magnesium sulphate

seedling grown with roots in culture solution providing selected ions at known, low concentrations, similar to those in a nutrient-rich soil solution

range of tubes set up:

complete culture solution minus N minus S minus P minus K minus Ca minus Mg minus Fe

cotton wool

air dissolves in culture solution

seedlings grown up in bulk and 8 selected of normal standardised size and shape

test tube covered by foil to exclude light (prevents growth of algae)

cultivated under favorable growing conditions (temperature, light regime, etc.)

plants inspected regularly for:
- general growth of plant
- shape of leaves
- length of leaf growth
- colour of upper leaves
- length of root growth
- colour of lower leaves

Extension: an alternative method of investigating essential ions

Lemna is a genus of aquatic floating plants that consist of tiny roots and small, green leaves. On stagnant fresh water this plant may form a green 'carpet' over the surface. A few may be harvested from their environment, the species identified, and then they may be used to study essential ions (Figure 2.22).

Figure 2.22 Using *Lemna* to investigate plant mineral nutrition.

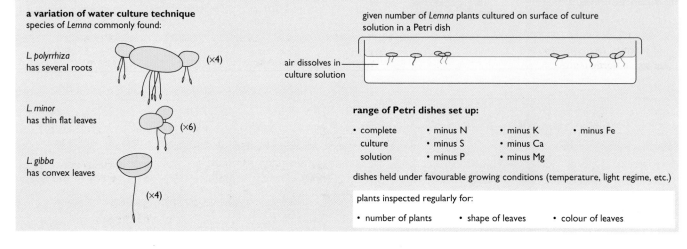

a variation of water culture technique
species of *Lemna* commonly found:

L. polyrrhiza has several roots (×4)

L. minor has thin flat leaves (×6)

L gibba has convex leaves (×4)

given number of *Lemna* plants cultured on surface of culture solution in a Petri dish

air dissolves in culture solution

range of Petri dishes set up:
- complete culture solution
- minus N
- minus S
- minus P
- minus K
- minus Ca
- minus Mg
- minus Fe

dishes held under favourable growing conditions (temperature, light regime, etc.)

plants inspected regularly for:
- number of plants
- shape of leaves
- colour of leaves

Signs and symptoms of ion deficiency

Plants grown deficient in an essential nutrient normally show characteristic signs and symptoms (Figure 2.23). When these symptoms appear in cultivated commercial crops, the mineral nutrients available in the soil may be checked by chemical analysis to confirm the deficiency. Then artificial fertiliser can be applied to make good the deficiency and restore normal growth patterns.

Figure 2.23 Symptoms of mineral deficiency in the tobacco plant.

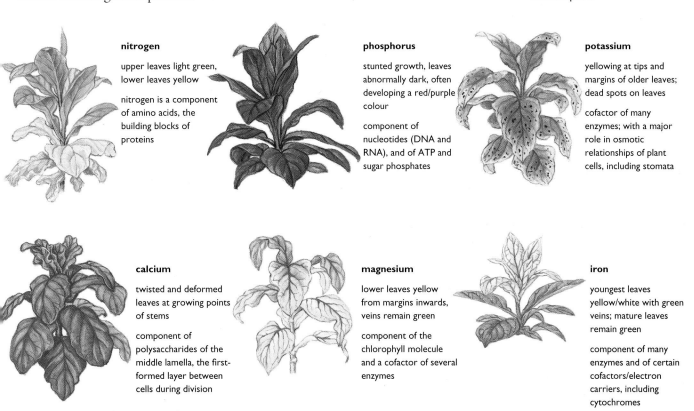

nitrogen

upper leaves light green, lower leaves yellow

nitrogen is a component of amino acids, the building blocks of proteins

phosphorus

stunted growth, leaves abnormally dark, often developing a red/purple colour

component of nucleotides (DNA and RNA), and of ATP and sugar phosphates

potassium

yellowing at tips and margins of older leaves; dead spots on leaves

cofactor of many enzymes; with a major role in osmotic relationships of plant cells, including stomata

calcium

twisted and deformed leaves at growing points of stems

component of polysaccharides of the middle lamella, the first-formed layer between cells during division

magnesium

lower leaves yellow from margins inwards, veins remain green

component of the chlorophyll molecule and a cofactor of several enzymes

iron

youngest leaves yellow/white with green veins; mature leaves remain green

component of many enzymes and of certain cofactors/electron carriers, including cytochromes

Where ions come from

In the soil, the ions dissolved in the soil solution come from the mineral skeleton of soils by chemical erosion, and by decay of the dead organic matter that is constantly being added to the soil (Figure 2.24).

Crops and cultivated plants are additionally supplied by chemical fertilisers (manufactured) or by manure or compost.

8 Why and how is the supply of essential ions maintained in soil in horticulture?

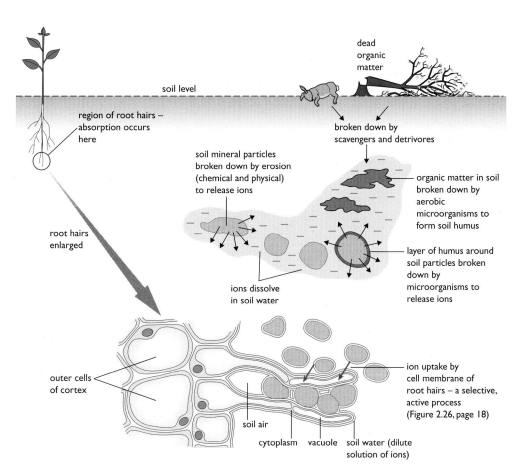

dead organic matter

soil level

region of root hairs – absorption occurs here

broken down by scavengers and detrivores

soil mineral particles broken down by erosion (chemical and physical) to release ions

organic matter in soil broken down by aerobic microorganisms to form soil humus

root hairs enlarged

layer of humus around soil particles broken down by microorganisms to release ions

ions dissolve in soil water

outer cells of cortex

ion uptake by cell membrane of root hairs – a selective, active process (Figure 2.26, page 18)

soil air

cytoplasm   vacuole   soil water (dilute solution of ions)

Figure 2.24 The sources of ions present in the soil solution, available to plants.

Availability and uptake of ions

The availability of ions in soils varies with the pH. Abnormally alkaline conditions make iron ions unavailable for uptake; and very acid conditions make calcium ions unavailable. This is due to reversible binding with insoluble soil mineral (mainly clay particles), taking particular ions out of solution over certain ranges of pH. This phenomenon is summarised in Figure 2.25.

Ion uptake is a **selective process** – for example, where nitrate and chloride ions are available, root hairs absorb more nitrate than chloride ions. Uptake is also an **active process**, involving energy from respiration (Figure 2.26). This is quite different from entry by diffusion, for example. Active uptake can (and frequently does) occur against a concentration gradient. Plant cells tend to hoard valuable ions such as nitrate and calcium ions, even when they are already at a higher concentration inside the cytoplasm.

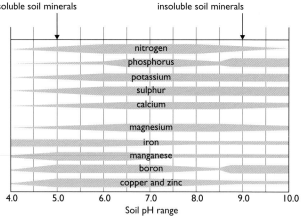

relative ion availability

at this pH, nitrates and other soluble forms of combined nitrogen are made insoluble through reactions with other insoluble soil minerals

at this pH, iron(II) ions and other soluble forms of iron are made insoluble through reactions with other insoluble soil minerals

Figure 2.25 Nutrient ion availability at different pH ranges.

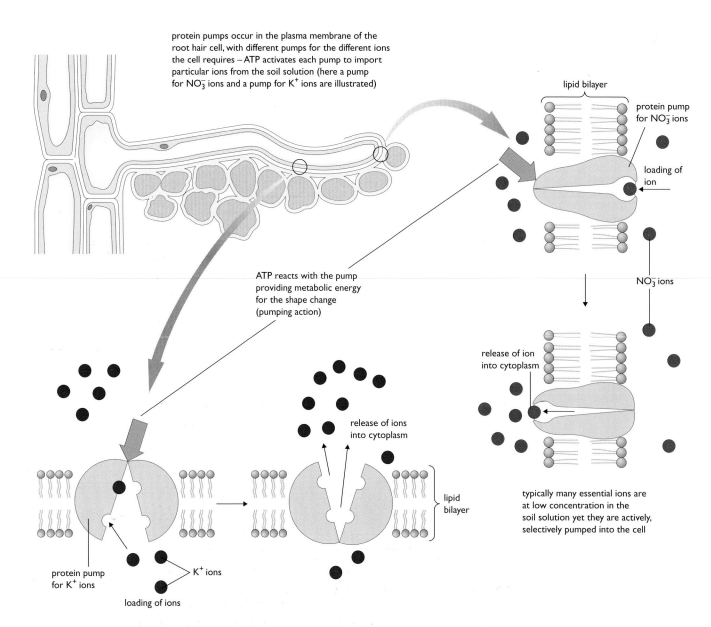

protein pumps occur in the plasma membrane of the root hair cell, with different pumps for the different ions the cell requires – ATP activates each pump to import particular ions from the soil solution (here a pump for NO_3^- ions and a pump for K^+ ions are illustrated)

lipid bilayer

protein pump for NO_3^- ions

loading of ion

NO_3^- ions

ATP reacts with the pump providing metabolic energy for the shape change (pumping action)

release of ion into cytoplasm

release of ions into cytoplasm

typically many essential ions are at low concentration in the soil solution yet they are actively, selectively pumped into the cell

lipid bilayer

protein pump for K^+ ions

K^+ ions

loading of ions

Figure 2.26 The active uptake of ions by protein pumps in root hair cell membranes.

Transport and metabolism of ions in the whole plant

Once absorption has occurred, ions are transported to different locations within the plant, to sites of use or storage (Figure 2.27). The essential nutrients required, and their chief roles in metabolism, are summarised in Table 2.2.

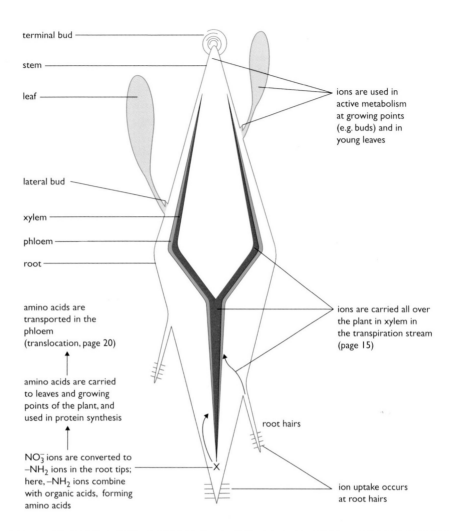

terminal bud

stem

leaf

lateral bud

xylem

phloem

root

ions are used in active metabolism at growing points (e.g. buds) and in young leaves

ions are carried all over the plant in xylem in the transpiration stream (page 15)

amino acids are transported in the phloem (translocation, page 20)

amino acids are carried to leaves and growing points of the plant, and used in protein synthesis

NO_3^- ions are converted to $-NH_2$ ions in the root tips; here, $-NH_2$ ions combine with organic acids, forming amino acids

root hairs

ion uptake occurs at root hairs

X

Figure 2.27 Movement of ions about the plant.

Table 2.2 Macro- and micronutrients essential for plant growth

Element	Form obtained by plants	Functions
Macronutrients:		
Nitrogen (N)	Nitrate and ammonium ions	Synthesis of proteins from amino acids; synthesis of many other important compounds e.g. chlorophyll, coenzymes
Phosphorus (P)	Phosphate ions	Synthesis of nucleic acids, ATP and phospholipids
Sulphur (S)	Sulphate ions	Synthesis of proteins, and in other compounds e.g. Coenzyme A
Calcium (Ca)	Calcium ions	Middle lamella formation between plant cells
Magnesium (Mg)	Magnesium ions	Part of the chlorophyll molecule; cofactor of many enzymes
Potassium (K)	Potassium ions	Involved with Na^+ in membrane function and in stomatal opening
Sodium (Na)	Sodium ions	Involved with potassium in membrane function
Chlorine (Cl)	Chloride ions	Osmotic relations of cells
Micronutrients:		
Iron (Fe)	Iron compounds	Part of electron-transport molecules, e.g. cytochromes; involved in chlorophyll synthesis
Manganese (Mn)	Manganese compounds	Component of specific enzymes
Copper (Cu)	Copper compounds	Activates specific enzymes; electron-transport molecules of photosynthesis
Cobalt (Co)	Cobalt compounds	As vitamin B_{12}; in cell division
Zinc (Zn)	Zinc compounds	Component of specific enzymes, e.g. alcohol dehydrogenase
Molybdenum (Mo)	Molybdenum compounds	Component of enzymes of amino acid synthesis, and of enzyme of nitrogen fixation in *Rhizobium* (bacterium)
Boron (B)	Boron compounds	Required in cell division process in plants

9 The diameter of a tree trunk, measured in summer months, decreases in the day but recovers in the night. Why does this happen?

Transport of nutrients in the plant

The movement of sugars and amino acids occurs in the phloem. This is known as **translocation**. Sugars, produced in leaves in the light, are carried to developing leaves, buds and meristems, and to sites of starch storage in stem and roots. Amino acids, synthesised in the root tips, are transported mainly to the growing points of the plant. So transport in the phloem tissue occurs both up and down the stem and roots – although not in both directions in individual sieve tubes. By contrast, water in xylem vessels flows only from roots to stem and leaves.

Phloem and xylem originate from cells of the procambial strand (page 10). Xylem vessels are empty tubes with lignin-thickened longitudinal walls. Phloem consists of living cells – the sieve tube elements and companion cells. Translocation is dependent on living cells (Figure 2.28), and there is a close relationship between sieve elements and their companion cells (Figure 2.29).

10 Contrast the changes undergone in a procambial strand cell as it matures into:
a) a xylem vessel
b) a sieve tube element.

Figure 2.28 Translocation requires living cells.

this is shown by investigation of the effect of temperature on phloem transport

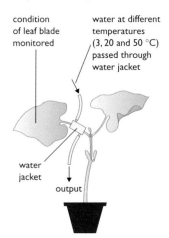

condition of leaf blade monitored

water at different temperatures (3, 20 and 50 °C) passed through water jacket

water jacket

output

(a) at 50 °C, translocation of sugar from the leaf blade stopped – this is above the thermal death point of cytoplasm

conclusion: living cells are essential for translocation

(b) at 3 °C, compared with 20 °C, translocation of sugar from leaf blade was reduced by almost 10% of leaf dry weight over a given time

conclusion: rate of metabolic activity of phloem cells affects rate of translocation

Note: in neither experiment did the leaf blade wilt – xylem transport is not heat-sensitive at this range of temperatures (because xylem vessels are dead, empty tubes)

companion cell and sieve tube element in LS (high power)

sieve plate in surface view

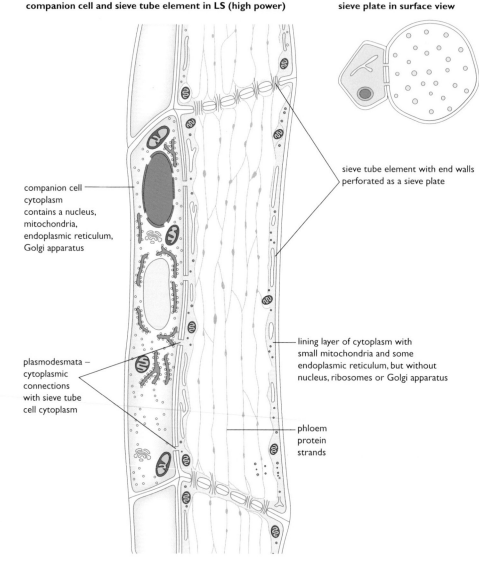

companion cell cytoplasm contains a nucleus, mitochondria, endoplasmic reticulum, Golgi apparatus

plasmodesmata – cytoplasmic connections with sieve tube cell cytoplasm

sieve tube element with end walls perforated as a sieve plate

lining layer of cytoplasm with small mitochondria and some endoplasmic reticulum, but without nucleus, ribosomes or Golgi apparatus

phloem protein strands

phloem tissue in TS (low power)

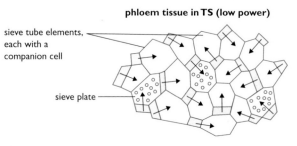

sieve tube elements, each with a companion cell

sieve plate

Figure 2.29 The fine structure of phloem tissue.

Investigating phloem transport

Movement of nutrients in the phloem has been investigated using radioactively labelled metabolites. ^{14}C-labelled sugars, manufactured in illuminated leaves 'fed' $^{14}CO_2$, can be traced during translocation. For example, the contents of individual sieve tubes can be sampled using the mouthparts of aphids as micropipettes, once these have been inserted into the plant by the insect (Figure 2.30).

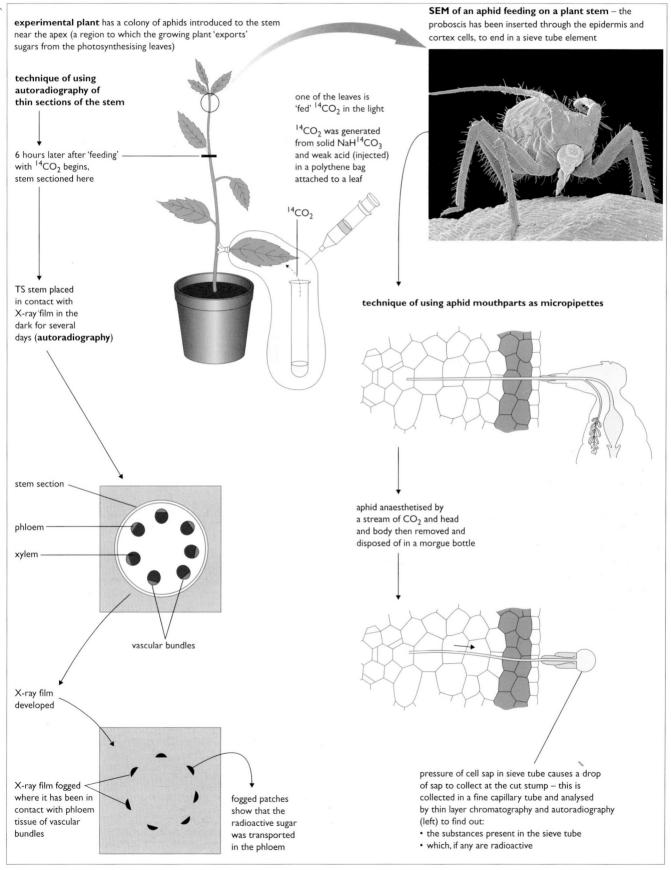

experimental plant has a colony of aphids introduced to the stem near the apex (a region to which the growing plant 'exports' sugars from the photosynthesising leaves)

technique of using autoradiography of thin sections of the stem

6 hours later after 'feeding' with $^{14}CO_2$ begins, stem sectioned here

TS stem placed in contact with X-ray film in the dark for several days (**autoradiography**)

one of the leaves is 'fed' $^{14}CO_2$ in the light

$^{14}CO_2$ was generated from solid $NaH^{14}CO_3$ and weak acid (injected) in a polythene bag attached to a leaf

$^{14}CO_2$

SEM of an aphid feeding on a plant stem – the proboscis has been inserted through the epidermis and cortex cells, to end in a sieve tube element

technique of using aphid mouthparts as micropipettes

aphid anaesthetised by a stream of CO_2 and head and body then removed and disposed of in a morgue bottle

stem section

phloem

xylem

vascular bundles

X-ray film developed

X-ray film fogged where it has been in contact with phloem tissue of vascular bundles

fogged patches show that the radioactive sugar was transported in the phloem

pressure of cell sap in sieve tube causes a drop of sap to collect at the cut stump – this is collected in a fine capillary tube and analysed by thin layer chromatography and autoradiography (left) to find out:
• the substances present in the sieve tube
• which, if any are radioactive

Figure 2.30 Using radioactive carbon to investigate phloem transport.

How are nutrients loaded into the sieve tube elements?

Sugars are loaded into the sieve tubes from the mesophyll cells (Figure 2.1, page 2) near the veins in leaves. This occurs via special parenchyma cells called **transfer cells** (Figure 2.31).

Figure 2.31 Transfer cells and the loading of phloem sieve tubes.

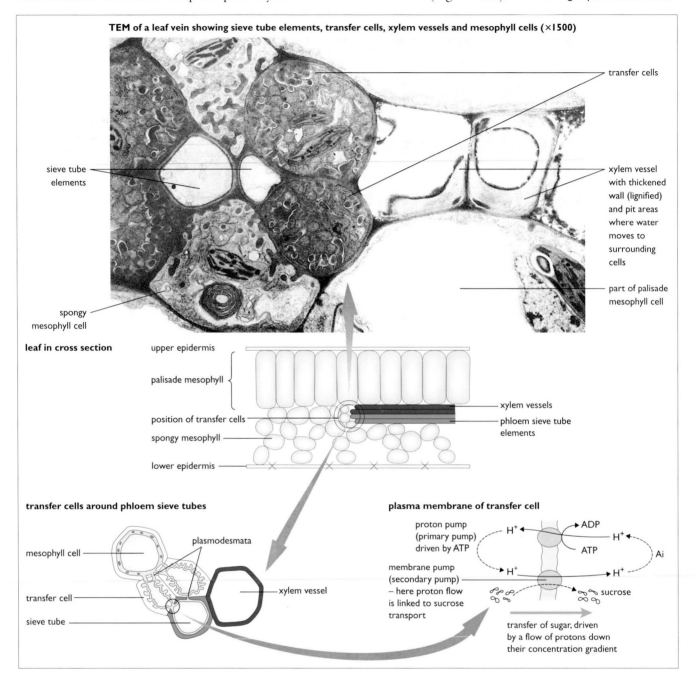

TEM of a leaf vein showing sieve tube elements, transfer cells, xylem vessels and mesophyll cells (×1500)

transfer cells

sieve tube elements

xylem vessel with thickened wall (lignified) and pit areas where water moves to surrounding cells

part of palisade mesophyll cell

spongy mesophyll cell

leaf in cross section

upper epidermis
palisade mesophyll
position of transfer cells
spongy mesophyll
lower epidermis

xylem vessels
phloem sieve tube elements

transfer cells around phloem sieve tubes

mesophyll cell
plasmodesmata
transfer cell
sieve tube
xylem vessel

plasma membrane of transfer cell

proton pump (primary pump) driven by ATP
membrane pump (secondary pump) – here proton flow is linked to sucrose transport

ADP
ATP
H^+
H^+
Ai
sucrose
transfer of sugar, driven by a flow of protons down their concentration gradient

Phloem transport – the movement of sugars in sieve tube elements

Subsequent to loading into the sieve tube elements, sugars (and other nutrients) are moved through the phloem at speeds of up to $100\,cm\,h^{-1}$. This is much faster than would occur by diffusion alone. How is phloem transport brought about? No single theory of phloem transport is fully accepted, but an important hypothesis, **pressure flow**, is illustrated opposite. Evidence for and against pressure flow is listed in Table 2.3.

11 In Figure 2.28, high temperature stopped phloem transport. How may heat have this effect?

Table 2.3 Evidence for and against pressure flow

For	Against
Contents of sieve tubes are under pressure, and sugar solution exudes if phloem is cut.	Phloem tissue carries manufactured food to various destinations simultaneously (in different sieve tubes), rather than to the greatest 'sink'
Appropriate gradients between 'source' and 'sink' tissues do exist	Sieve plates are a barrier to mass flow, and might be expected to have been 'lost' in the course of evolution if mass flow is the mechanism of phloem transport

The pressure flow hypothesis of phloem transport

The principle of the pressure flow hypothesis is that the sugar solution flows down a hydrostatic pressure gradient. There is a high hydrostatic pressure in sieve tube elements near mesophyll cells in the light, but low hydrostatic pressure in elements near starch storage cells of stem and root (Figure 2.32).

In this hypothesis, the role of the companion cells (living cells with a full range of organelles in the cytoplasm) is to maintain conditions in the sieve tube elements favourable to mass flow of solutes. Companion cells use metabolic energy (ATP) to do this.

Figure 2.32 The pressure flow theory of phloem transport.

model demonstrating pressure flow
(A ≡ mesophyll cell, B ≡ starch storage cell)

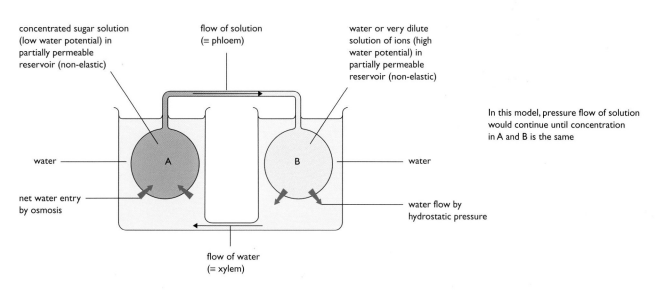

concentrated sugar solution (low water potential) in partially permeable reservoir (non-elastic)

flow of solution (≡ phloem)

water or very dilute solution of ions (high water potential) in partially permeable reservoir (non-elastic)

In this model, pressure flow of solution would continue until concentration in A and B is the same

water

A

B

water

net water entry by osmosis

water flow by hydrostatic pressure

flow of water (≡ xylem)

pressure flow in the plant

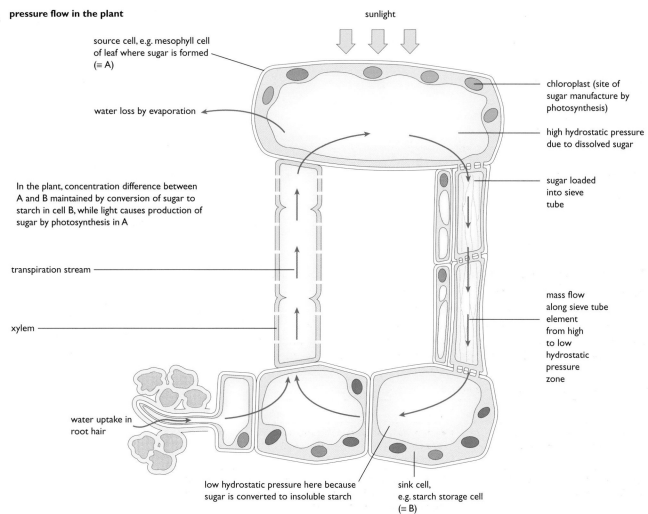

sunlight

source cell, e.g. mesophyll cell of leaf where sugar is formed (≡ A)

chloroplast (site of sugar manufacture by photosynthesis)

water loss by evaporation

high hydrostatic pressure due to dissolved sugar

In the plant, concentration difference between A and B maintained by conversion of sugar to starch in cell B, while light causes production of sugar by photosynthesis in A

sugar loaded into sieve tube

transpiration stream

xylem

mass flow along sieve tube element from high to low hydrostatic pressure zone

water uptake in root hair

low hydrostatic pressure here because sugar is converted to insoluble starch

sink cell, e.g. starch storage cell (≡ B)

The nutrition of green plants, **autotrophic nutrition** (Figure 2.2, page 3), is sustained by photosynthesis. Sugar from photosynthesis provides the carbon 'skeletons' for the synthesis of all the biochemicals and metabolites the plant needs. Respiration of sugar, together with photosynthesis itself (Figure 3.18, page 32), provides energy (as ATP) for the reactions of synthesis, and to drive the activities of plants. This chapter is about the process of photosynthesis in plants. Photosynthesis is of significance for the whole living world. The extent of photosynthesis, and aspects of its effects on the composition of the atmosphere, are evident from the carbon cycle (Figure 3.1). Feeding relationships (food webs) demonstrate the dependence of all other organisms on plants or the products of plants, directly or indirectly (Figure 3.2).

I What is the fate of 90% of the food matter eaten by a carnivore (e.g. of a caterpillar eaten by shrew)?

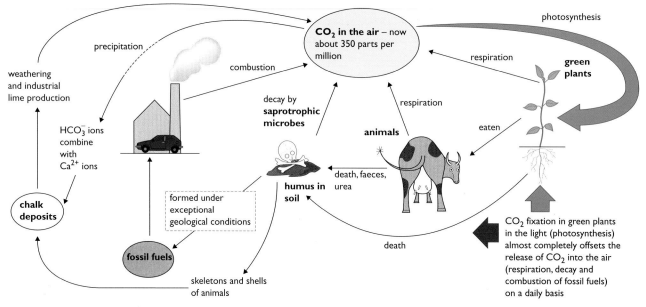

Figure 3.1 The carbon cycle.

only about 10% of the energy taken up by an organism at one level of the food chain is turned into tissue and so is potentially available to the browser or predator feeding on that organism – so feeding relationships are structured like a pyramid of biomass

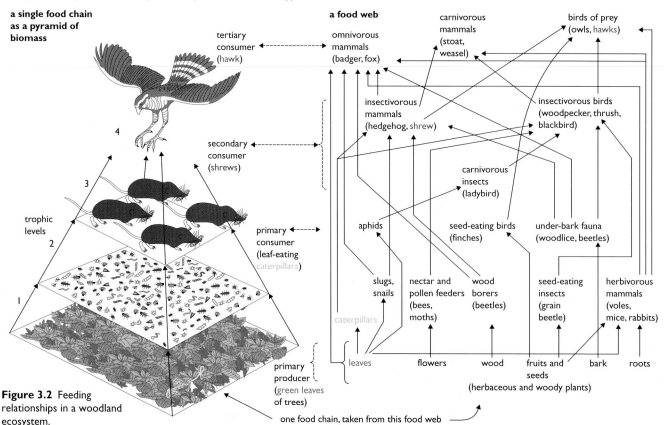

Figure 3.2 Feeding relationships in a woodland ecosystem.

Chloroplasts – site of photosynthesis

Chloroplasts are one of the larger organelles found in plant cells, yet they typically measure only 4–10 µm long and 2–3 µm wide. (A µm (micron) is $^1/_{1\,000\,000}$ of a mm (millimetre).) Consequently, while chloroplasts can be seen in outline by light microscopy, for the detail of fine structure (ultrastructure), electron microscopy is used. A transmission electron micrograph (TEM) is produced from thin sections of mesophyll cells, specially prepared (Figure 3.3). This is necessary because the electron beam travels at high speed, but at low energy. Air molecules would deflect this beam, so the inside of the microscope is a vacuum. Consequently, living material must first be killed, then 'fixed' in a life-like condition and dehydrated (water would boil away in a vacuum). Specimens must be thin for electrons to pass through at all, so thin sections are cut and then stained with electron-dense salts to increase the contrast.

Figure 3.3 The production of a TEM of chloroplasts.

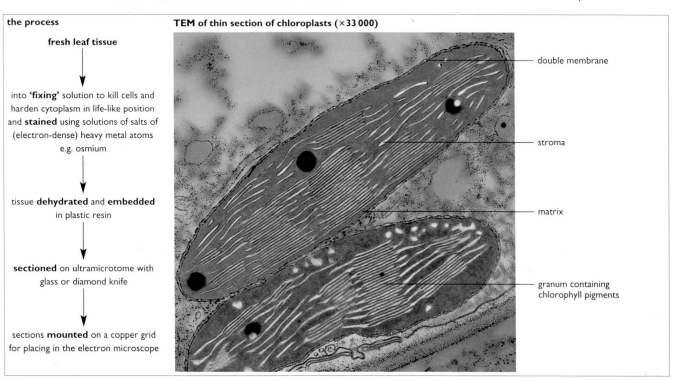

the process

fresh leaf tissue

into **'fixing'** solution to kill cells and harden cytoplasm in life-like position and **stained** using solutions of salts of (electron-dense) heavy metal atoms e.g. osmium

tissue **dehydrated** and **embedded** in plastic resin

sectioned on ultramicrotome with glass or diamond knife

sections **mounted** on a copper grid for placing in the electron microscope

TEM of thin section of chloroplasts (×33 000)

double membrane

stroma

matrix

granum containing chlorophyll pigments

The ultrastructure of chloroplasts

A chloroplast has a double membrane (Figure 3.4). The outer membrane is a continuous boundary, but the inner 'in-tucks' to form branching membranes called lamellae or thylakoids that occupy the centre of the organelle. Some of the thylakoids are arranged in circular piles called **grana**. Here the photosynthetic pigment chlorophyll is held. Between the grana, the lamellae are loosely arranged in an aqueous matrix, forming the **stroma**. Chloroplasts are members of a group of organelles called plastids. Other plastids include leucoplasts, the sites of starch storage in plant cells.

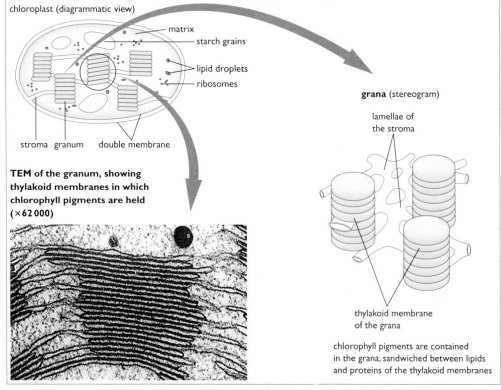

chloroplast (diagrammatic view)

matrix
starch grains
lipid droplets
ribosomes

stroma   granum   double membrane

TEM of the granum, showing thylakoid membranes in which chlorophyll pigments are held (×62 000)

grana (stereogram)

lamellae of the stroma

thylakoid membrane of the grana

chlorophyll pigments are contained in the grana, sandwiched between lipids and proteins of the thylakoid membranes

Figure 3.4 The ultrastructure of a chloroplast.

Investigating chlorophyll

Photosynthetic organisms contain chlorophyll, located within the grana of chloroplasts. *In situ*, when activated by absorption of light energy these organic molecules bring about the photochemical steps of photosynthesis (page 32). Chlorophyll can be extracted from leaves in order to investigate its composition and properties. These pigments are not water-soluble, but dissolve in certain organic solvents (Figure 3.5), and can be separated by chromatography (Figures 3.6 and 3.7).

Figure 3.5 Steps in the extraction of chlorophyll.

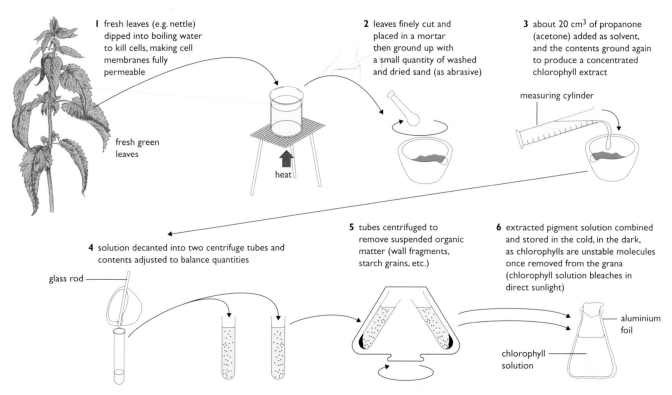

1 fresh leaves (e.g. nettle) dipped into boiling water to kill cells, making cell membranes fully permeable

fresh green leaves

heat

2 leaves finely cut and placed in a mortar then ground up with a small quantity of washed and dried sand (as abrasive)

3 about 20 cm³ of propanone (acetone) added as solvent, and the contents ground again to produce a concentrated chlorophyll extract

measuring cylinder

4 solution decanted into two centrifuge tubes and contents adjusted to balance quantities

glass rod

5 tubes centrifuged to remove suspended organic matter (wall fragments, starch grains, etc.)

6 extracted pigment solution combined and stored in the cold, in the dark, as chlorophylls are unstable molecules once removed from the grana (chlorophyll solution bleaches in direct sunlight)

aluminium foil

chlorophyll solution

Figure 3.6 Separation of chlorophyll pigments by thin-layer or paper chromatography.

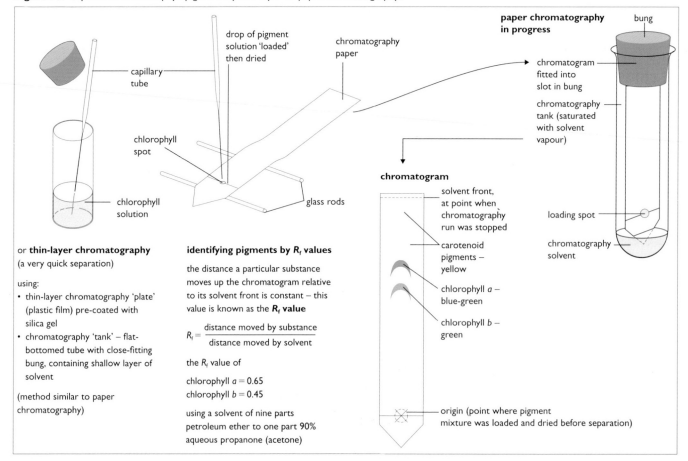

capillary tube

drop of pigment solution 'loaded' then dried

chromatography paper

paper chromatography in progress   bung

chromatogram fitted into slot in bung

chromatography tank (saturated with solvent vapour)

chlorophyll spot

chlorophyll solution

glass rods

chromatogram

solvent front, at point when chromatography run was stopped

carotenoid pigments – yellow

chlorophyll *a* – blue-green

chlorophyll *b* – green

loading spot

chromatography solvent

origin (point where pigment mixture was loaded and dried before separation)

or **thin-layer chromatography** (a very quick separation)

using:
- thin-layer chromatography 'plate' (plastic film) pre-coated with silica gel
- chromatography 'tank' – flat-bottomed tube with close-fitting bung, containing shallow layer of solvent

(method similar to paper chromatography)

identifying pigments by R_f values

the distance a particular substance moves up the chromatogram relative to its solvent front is constant – this value is known as the **R_f value**

$$R_f = \frac{\text{distance moved by substance}}{\text{distance moved by solvent}}$$

the R_f value of

chlorophyll $a = 0.65$
chlorophyll $b = 0.45$

using a solvent of nine parts petroleum ether to one part 90% aqueous propanone (acetone)

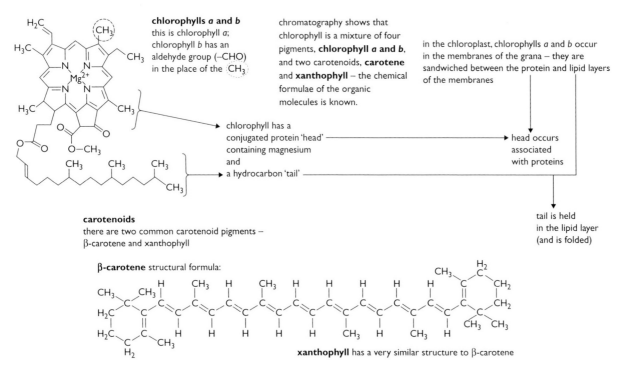

Figure 3.7 The component pigments of green plant chlorophyll.

Light absorption and photosynthesis

Chlorophyll does not absorb green light; this wavelength is transmitted. The components of white light that chlorophyll absorbs (its **absorption spectrum**) are found by measuring the absorption of different wavelengths by solutions of chlorophyll pigments, after they have been separated (for example, by column chromatography). The results are plotted as a graph of light absorption against wavelength.

The components of white light that bring about photosynthesis (the **action spectrum**; Figure 3.8) may be discovered by projecting different wavelengths, in turn and for a unit of time, on aquatic green pondweed as shown in Figure 3.10 (page 28). The results are plotted as a graph of the rate of photosynthesis (as rate of oxygen production) against wavelengths.

2 What safety precautions are essential in chlorophyll extractions?

absorption spectrum
measured using a spectrometer

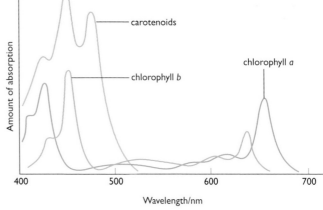

action spectrum
record of amount of photosynthesis occurring at each wavelength

results show that the wavelengths of light absorbed by photosynthetic pigments (largely red and blue) are very similar to the wavelengths that drive photosynthesis

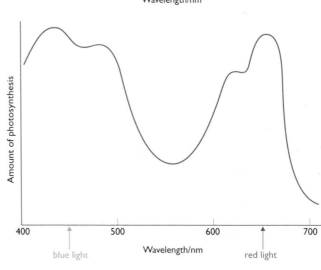

Figure 3.8 Absorption and action spectra of chlorophyll pigments.

Measuring the rate of photosynthesis

Investigating the effects of environmental factors on the rate of the process is one way to learn about photosynthesis.

Using Canadian pondweed (*Elodea canadensis*)

The rate of photosynthesis, recorded as oxygen produced in a given time under controlled conditions, may be measured using an aquatic plant such as *Elodea* – the oxygen evolved is collected by downward displacement of water. Plants adapted to submerged aquatic conditions retain the oxygen they produce (page 78), causing their leaves to float near the surface of the water. Here, chloroplasts are well illuminated during daylight. As *Elodea* retains oxygen in air spaces in its stem, its cut stems must be inverted in the water for the oxygen to be released as it is produced (Figures 3.9 and 3.10).

Figure 3.9 Photosynthesis in *Elodea*.

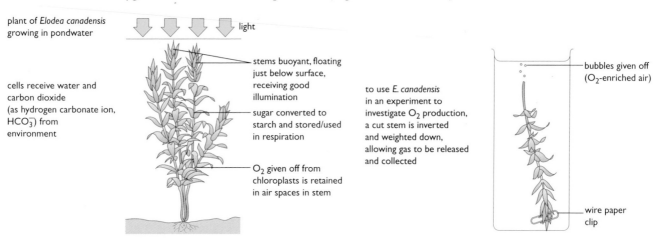

Photosynthesis apparatus

A simple photosynthometer exploits plants such as *Elodea*, and can be used to investigate the effects on the rate of photosynthesis of environmental factors such as light intensity, CO_2 concentration and temperature (Figure 3.10).

Figure 3.10 Using *Elodea* for rate determination experiments.

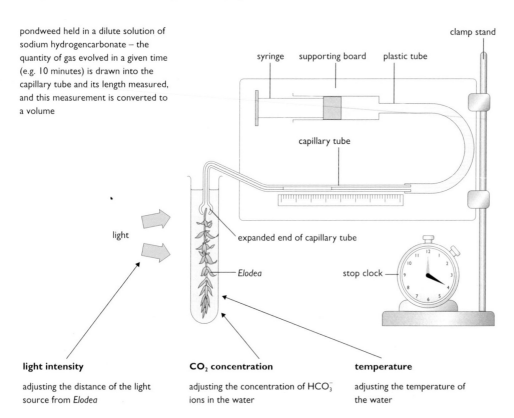

light intensity

adjusting the distance of the light source from *Elodea*

CO_2 concentration

adjusting the concentration of HCO_3^- ions in the water

temperature

adjusting the temperature of the water

the external factors are varied and their effects on oxygen released measured, but the *Elodea* must be allowed to adapt to the new conditions each time they are changed before readings are recorded

Extension: using an oxygen electrode – the research laboratory approach

The oxygen electrode (Figure 3.11) is an especially accurate instrument for measuring the partial pressure of oxygen in a suspension of *Chlorella* cells (page 33), or of isolated chloroplasts. In this instrument, the electrode compartment is separated from the suspension by a membrane fully permeable to dissolved oxygen. With a voltage applied to the electrodes, current flow varies in linear relationship to the partial pressure of dissolved oxygen present. This current flow is measured by a meter with a scale calibrated in partial pressures of oxygen. The suspension is constantly stirred, so changes in oxygen production, for example as light intensity or CO_2 concentration are varied, are detected.

Figure 3.11 The oxygen electrode and measurement of the rate of photosynthesis.

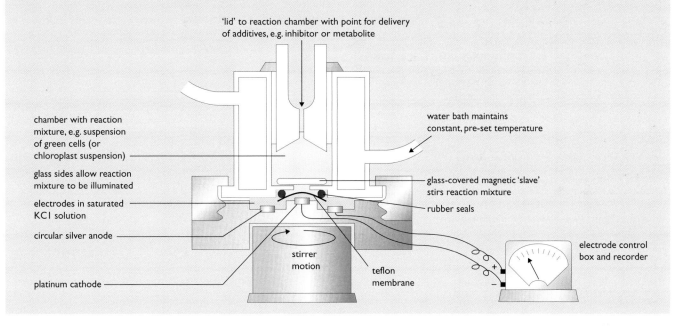

'lid' to reaction chamber with point for delivery of additives, e.g. inhibitor or metabolite

chamber with reaction mixture, e.g. suspension of green cells (or chloroplast suspension)

water bath maintains constant, pre-set temperature

glass sides allow reaction mixture to be illuminated

glass-covered magnetic 'slave' stirs reaction mixture

electrodes in saturated KCl solution

rubber seals

circular silver anode

stirrer motion

electrode control box and recorder

platinum cathode

teflon membrane

Photosynthesis and light intensity (investigated via the oxygen electrode)

The effect of varying light intensity on photosynthesis is illustrated in Figure 3.12.

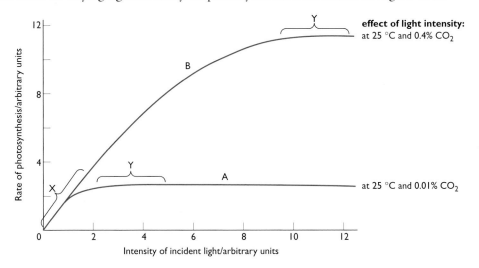

effect of light intensity:
at 25 °C and 0.4% CO_2

at 25 °C and 0.01% CO_2

Rate of photosynthesis/arbitrary units

Intensity of incident light/arbitrary units

Figure 3.12 Investigating effects of light intensity.

At low light intensities, the rate of photosynthesis increases linearly with increasing light – region X on the curves. Here the low light intensity (lack of sufficient light) is limiting photosynthesis. However, as light intensity is raised further, increasing light intensity produces no further effect on the rate of photosynthesis – region Y on the curves. Here, some factor other than light is limiting photosynthesis. What do you think may now be rate-limiting?

The limiting factor in region Y is disclosed when the investigation is repeated at higher CO_2 concentration (curve B). Here, the point when light intensity limits the rate of photosynthesis is also raised. So at higher light intensities the CO_2 concentration limits the rate of photosynthesis. Clearly, both light intensity and CO_2 concentration can be **limiting factors** in photosynthesis.

3 An oxygen electrode permits photosynthesis in chloroplasts to be measured. What are the likely advantages of this apparatus compared to measurements using a simple photosynthometer?

Photosynthesis and CO₂

Plant cells normally respire aerobically, releasing energy from sugar for the processes of life:

$$\text{glucose} + \text{oxygen} \rightarrow \text{waste products} + \text{energy.}$$
$$C_6H_{12}O_6 + 6O_2 \rightarrow 6CO_2 + 6H_2O + \text{about 32 ATPs}$$

ATP is the energy currency molecule of living things.

So in respiration the gas carbon dioxide is a waste product, and is given off, in contrast to its role in photosynthesis. Respiration continues in all cells, whether in the light or dark. However, in cells with chloroplasts (such as *Chlorella* and mesophyll cells) in full light, respiration is masked by photosynthesis:

$$6CO_2 + 6H_2O$$
photosynthesis   respiration
$$C_6H_{12}O_6 + 6O_2$$

This effect of light intensity on net exchange of carbon dioxide can be demonstrated (Figure 3.13).

Figure 3.13 The effect of light intensity on the net movement of carbon dioxide.

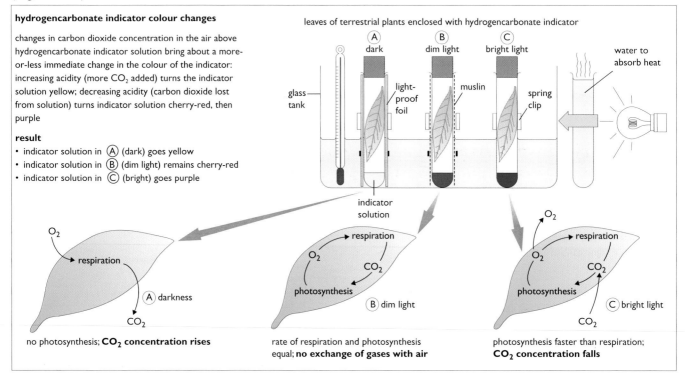

hydrogencarbonate indicator colour changes

changes in carbon dioxide concentration in the air above hydrogencarbonate indicator solution bring about a more-or-less immediate change in the colour of the indicator: increasing acidity (more CO_2 added) turns the indicator solution yellow; decreasing acidity (carbon dioxide lost from solution) turns indicator solution cherry-red, then purple

result
- indicator solution in Ⓐ (dark) goes yellow
- indicator solution in Ⓑ (dim light) remains cherry-red
- indicator solution in Ⓒ (bright) goes purple

leaves of terrestrial plants enclosed with hydrogencarbonate indicator

Ⓐ dark   Ⓑ dim light   Ⓒ bright light   water to absorb heat

glass tank   light-proof foil   muslin   spring clip

indicator solution

no photosynthesis; **CO₂ concentration rises**

rate of respiration and photosynthesis equal; **no exchange of gases with air**

photosynthesis faster than respiration; **CO₂ concentration falls**

Compensation point

The light intensity at which gas exchanges (CO_2 and O_2) due to photosynthesis and respiration are balanced is the **compensation point**. At higher light intensity, the green cell becomes a net importer of carbon dioxide – and a net exporter of oxygen (Figure 3.14).

photosynthesis and **respiration** are processes that can change the composition of the air; they also affect the amount of sugar held in the plant for use in metabolism

in darkness, a green plant cannot photosynthesise but respiration continues → as light intensity increases in the daylight, so does the rate of photosynthesis → eventually the compensation point is reached when all the CO_2 produced in respiration by the plant is re-used in photosynthesis, and there is no net loss or gain in CO_2

similarly, the plant uses up sugar reserves in the dark, but in full sunlight, carbohydrate reserves are built up

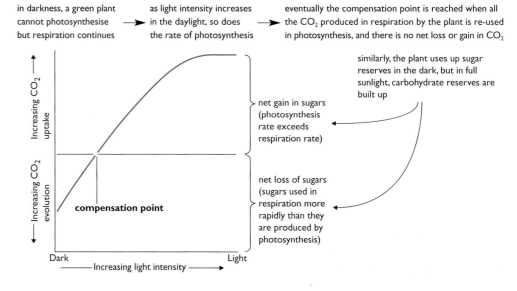

net gain in sugars (photosynthesis rate exceeds respiration rate)

net loss of sugars (sugars used in respiration more rapidly than they are produced by photosynthesis)

compensation point

Dark ——— Increasing light intensity ——— Light

Increasing CO₂ uptake / Increasing CO₂ evolution

Figure 3.14 Light intensity and the compensation point.

Effect of temperature on the rate of photosynthesis

Investigation of the effect of temperature on the rate of photosynthesis led to the discovery of two steps (reactions) to photosynthesis. This arose from the observation that the impact on photosynthesising cells of increasing temperature (e.g. from 10 to 30 °C) depends on the light intensity (Figure 3.15).

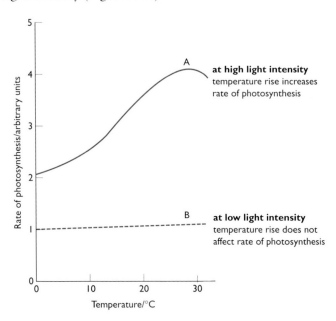

at high light intensity temperature rise increases rate of photosynthesis

at low light intensity temperature rise does not affect rate of photosynthesis

Figure 3.15 The effect of temperature on the rate of photosynthesis.

Extension: photosynthesis as a two-step process?

If photosynthesis includes a **photochemical reaction** (a temperature-insensitive change brought about by light energy), then when this reaction is rate-limiting (at low light intensity) a rise in temperature should not have a significant effect. This is what happens – Figure 3.15 (curve B).

If photosynthesis also includes **enzymic reactions** (temperature-sensitive changes involving enzymes), then when these reactions are rate-limiting (at high light intensity), a rise in temperature should have a significant effect. This, too, is what happens – Figure 3.15 (curve A).

This outcome is best explained if photosynthesis is made up of two sequential reactions (Figure 3.16).

- **A light-dependent reaction** – a photochemical step that, like all photochemical reactions, is unaffected by temperature. This might involve the splitting of water by light energy, releasing oxygen as a waste product (page 32).

- **A light-independent reaction** – a biochemical reaction that is catalysed by enzymes and is highly temperature-sensitive. This might involve the 'fixing' of carbon dioxide to form sugar. This hypothesis has since been confirmed by biochemical investigations (page 33).

4 Why is it important to control temperature when we develop a photographic film – but not when we take the picture?

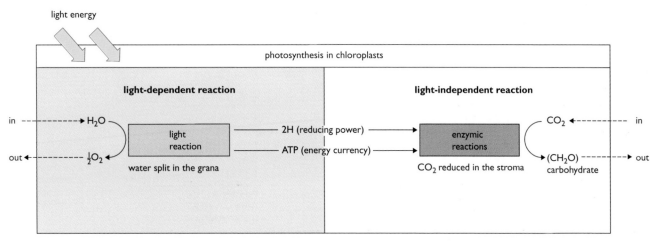

Figure 3.16 The two reactions to photosynthesis.

The light-dependent reaction

In the light-dependent stage, light energy is trapped by photosynthetic pigments arranged in **photosystems**, present in the **grana** (Figure 3.17). Here, many pigment molecules harvest light energy and funnel it into a special chlorophyll molecule at the **reaction centre** of the photosystem. One type of reaction centre is activated by light of wavelength 700 nm (in photosystem I); the other by light energy of wavelength 680 nm (in photosystem II). Photosystems are grouped together in the **thylakoid membranes** of the grana, together with specific proteins that are:

- **enzymes,** catalysing the
  - splitting of water into hydrogen ions, electrons and oxygen atoms
  - formation of ATP (energy currency molecules) from ADP and phosphate (P_i)
  - conversion of oxidised H-carrier (NADP) to reduced carrier ($NADPH_2$)
- **electron carrier molecules**.

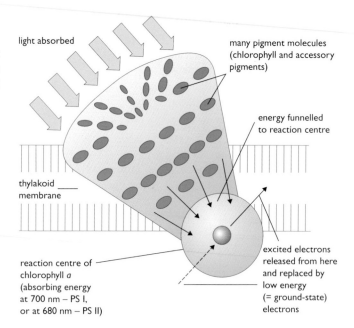

Figure 3.17 The structure of photosystems.

In the **light-dependent reaction**, light energy funnelled to the reaction centres excites and temporarily displaces particular electrons (Figure 3.18). Displaced electrons are replaced by electrons in the ground state. As a result, the splitting of water and release of O_2 gas occurs, and a head of hydrogen ions builds up within the thylakoid space. Also, reduced hydrogen acceptor molecules ($NADPH_2$) are formed. The synthesis of ATP from ADP and phosphate is driven by the hydrogen ions trapped within the thylakoid space, as these flow out via ATPase enzymes down an electrochemical gradient.

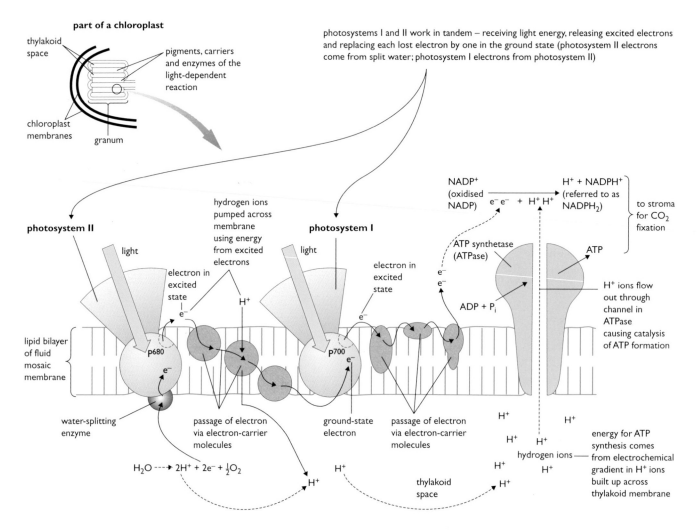

Figure 3.18 The light-dependent reaction.

The light-independent reaction

Finding the pathway of carbon in photosynthesis

The conversion of CO_2 into the products of photosynthesis has been investigated by 'feeding' experiments using radioactively labelled CO_2 (Figure 3.19). $^{14}CO_2$ is taken up by the cells and is fixed into the products of photosynthesis, in just the same way as unlabelled (^{12}C) carbon dioxide. Samples of the photosynthesising cells, taken at frequent intervals after a 'pulse' of $^{14}CO_2$ had been fed, contained a sequence of radioactively labelled intermediates and (later) products of the photosynthetic pathway. These compounds were isolated by chromatography from the sampled cells and identified. A culture of *Chlorella*, a unicellular alga, was used in this experiment in place of mesophyll cells, as they have identical photosynthesis and allow easy sampling.

5 Why is only a brief pulse of $^{14}CO_2$ fed in an investigation of the C-pathway of photosynthesis?

Figure 3.19 Investigation of the light-independent reactions of photosynthesis.

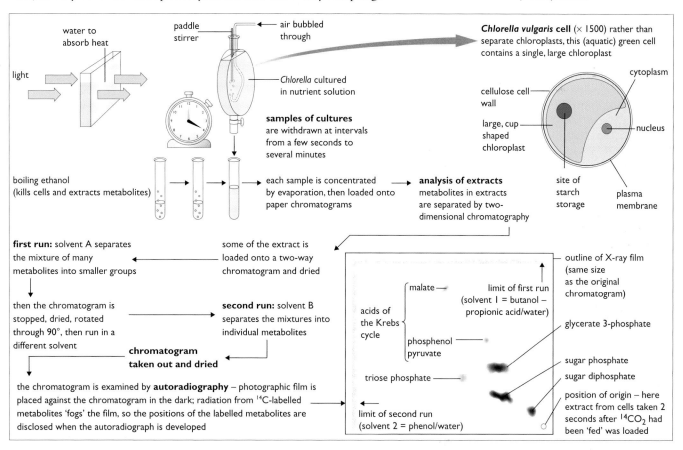

The carbon pathway of photosynthesis – in summary

Carbon dioxide is combined with a five-carbon acceptor molecule (ribulose bisphosphate) in the presence of the enzyme **Rubisco** (ribulose bisphosphate carboxylase). The products are **three-carbon sugars** (glycerate-3-phosphate, then triose phosphate). From these, other sugars, with starch and various lipids and amino acids, are formed together with more acceptor molecules. These reactions require a supply of ATP and $NADPH_2$ from the light-dependent reaction.

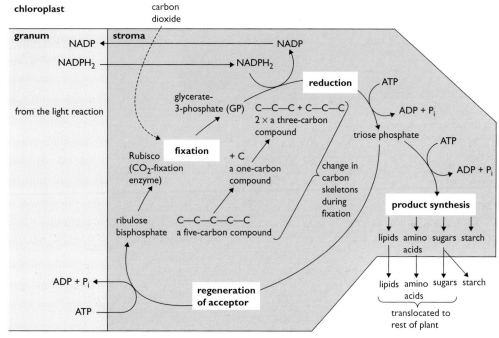

Figure 3.20 A summary of the path of carbon in photosynthesis.

Reproduction, life cycles and genetic modification

Flowering plants and flowers

Flowering plants are the most successful terrestrial plants. There are more species of them, and they dominate in many more habitats, than any other group of green plants. We identify flowering plants by their unique feature – flowers. From flowers come seeds, which grow to form new individuals similar, but not identical, to the parent plants. Seeds are the products of sexual reproduction in the life cycle of the flowering plant (page 44). One of the many reasons for the success of flowering plants is their relationship with animal life. Plants have evolved strategies of attracting animals to their flowers, feeding the visitors, and exploiting animal mobility in pollination (page 41) and seed dispersal (page 43).

Introducing flower structure

The flower develops at the tip of a shoot, and the parts of flowers may be seen as modified leaves. We are ignorant of the evolutionary history of the flower. However, we do know that environmental signals trigger a vegetative shoot to switch to flower production (page 74). The result is the formation of either a **solitary** flower on a stalk (such as a poppy), or a group of flowers on a main stem, called an **inflorescence** (Figure 4.3). The parts that make up a flower are borne on the expanded stem tip, the **receptacle**. The **sepals** (collectively the **calyx**) enclose the flower in the bud, and are usually small, green and leaf-like. The **petals** (collectively the **corolla**) are coloured and conspicuous, and may attract insects. The **stamens** (androecium – the male parts of the flower) consist of **anthers** (housing **pollen grains**) and a stalk or **filament**. The **carpels** (gynoecium – the female parts of the flower) may be one or many, free-standing or fused together. Each consists of an **ovary** (containing ovules); **stigma** (surface receiving pollen); and a connecting **style**. The buttercup flower is shown in Figure 4.1.

1 What are the nutritional advantages to a bee of visiting a buttercup flower?

Figure 4.1 Structure of the buttercup flower.

buttercups – a habitat view

buttercup flowers occur in an inflorescence

youngest flower

oldest flower

inflorescence

bract

flower stalk

half flower of *Ranunculus* sp. (buttercup)

petal

a plan drawing or floral diagram of the buttercup flower (here the parts are represented in transverse section)

carpel showing { stigma / style / ovary }

sepal

nectary
receptacle

anther
filament } stamen

flower stalk

lower down the flower stalk is a leaf-like bract – see inflorescence view

The irregular flowers

The buttercup flower is **regular** or **radially symmetrical** – it can be cut into identical halves along many radii. Not all flowers are like this. For example, the white dead nettle flower is **irregular** or **bilaterally symmetrical** – only one plane cuts the flower into identical halves. It also has sepals and petals partially fused together into tubes, and the petals curve over, almost like an umbrella. As a result, the centre is protected from rain and only insects with a relatively long proboscis (such as bees) are equipped to feed in the flower (Figure 4.2). By contrast, the centre of the buttercup flower is open to many visitors, such as insects that climb the stalk and pass between the sepals and petals, and those that fly in. Also, the nectar is unprotected from rain.

Figure 4.2 The white dead nettle flower.

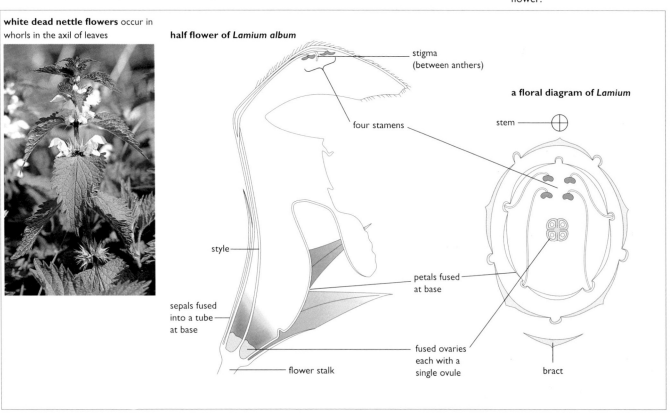

white dead nettle flowers occur in whorls in the axil of leaves

half flower of *Lamium album*

stigma (between anthers)

four stamens

style

sepals fused into a tube at base

flower stalk

petals fused at base

fused ovaries each with a single ovule

a floral diagram of *Lamium*

stem

bract

Extension: looking at the arrangement of flowers in the inflorescence

A large, solitary flower can be seen as an uneconomical investment, compared with a group of smaller flowers grouped together compactly. The latter can be equally conspicuous, attracting many insect visitors which each serve many flowers of the inflorescence (Figure 4.3).

Figure 4.3 Arrangements of flowers in inflorescences.

simple raceme
e.g. toadflax

spike
e.g. mullein

umbel
e.g. cow parsley

composite head/capitulum
e.g. hawkbit

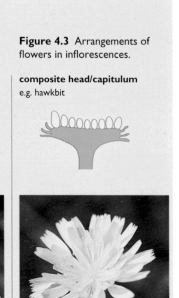

Dicotyledons, monocotyledons and flower structure

The flowering plants consist of the **dicotyledons** and the **monocotyledons**. This division is based on distinctive floral and vegetative characteristics, listed in Table 4.1.

Table 4.1 Differences between dicotyledons and monocotyledons

Character	Monocotyledons (e.g. iris, maize, grasses such as *Lolium*)	Dicotyledons (e.g. buttercup, white dead nettle)
Number of seed leaves (cotyledons – page 42)	One	Two
Leaf shape/venation	Typically bayonet- or strap-shaped leaves with parallel veins	Typically broad leaves with a network of veins
Flower parts (sepals/petals/stamens/carpels)	Have flower parts in threes (or in multiples of three)	Typically have flower parts in twos (or multiples), or in fives
Arrangement of vascular bundles in stem	Vascular bundles numerous, scattered throughout stem	Vascular bundles arranged in a ring, near outside of stem
Cambium (cells capable of further cell division, found in vascular bundles)	Mature vascular bundles without cambium; typically monocots show no secondary thickening (woody structures) – but the palm trees are an exception	Mature vascular bundles have a line of cambium between phloem (outside) and xylem (inside); plant may show secondary thickening (page 11)

The structure of monocotyledonous flowers

Lily and iris

These plants are examples of monocotyledons with showy flowers that are attractive to insects. The flower parts occur in threes or multiples of three. Sepals and petals are petaloid, and called the perianth.

Figure 4.4 Two insect-pollinated, monocotyledonous flowers.

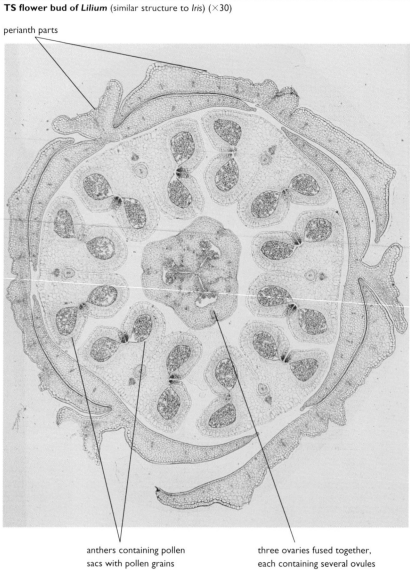

TS flower bud of *Lilium* (similar structure to *Iris*) (×30)

perianth parts

yellow iris (*Iris pseudacorus*) plant growing in a freshwater marsh

anthers containing pollen sacs with pollen grains

three ovaries fused together, each containing several ovules

Grasses – A huge family within the monocotyledons

The grasses are of great economic importance (page 50). Many are cultivated species, bred to serve as fodder for animals or as a source of grains for humans and animals. Grasses are wind-pollinated plants, so their flowers are typically inconspicuous (Figure 4.12, page 41). However, for effective wind pollination, huge quantities of pollen are produced and released into the air. This pollen often triggers allergic disease (hay fever) in humans.

2 What are the structural differences between the leaves of the buttercup and ryegrass?

Figure 4.5 Grasses typical of different soils.

Figure 4.6 The structure of perennial rye-grass (*Lolium perenne*).

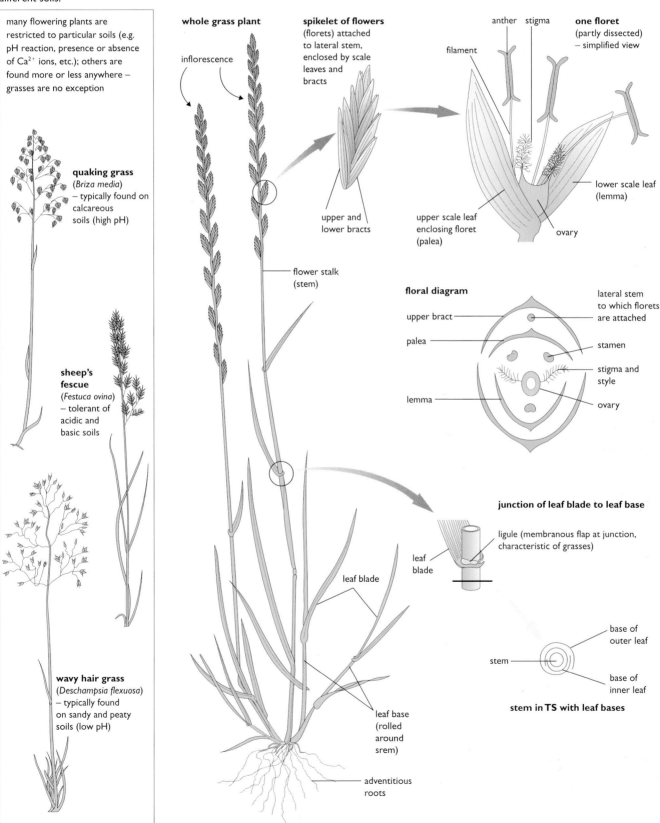

many flowering plants are restricted to particular soils (e.g. pH reaction, presence or absence of Ca^{2+} ions, etc.); others are found more or less anywhere – grasses are no exception

quaking grass
(*Briza media*)
– typically found on calcareous soils (high pH)

sheep's fescue
(*Festuca ovina*)
– tolerant of acidic and basic soils

wavy hair grass
(*Deschampsia flexuosa*)
– typically found on sandy and peaty soils (low pH)

whole grass plant

inflorescence

spikelet of flowers
(florets) attached to lateral stem, enclosed by scale leaves and bracts

upper and lower bracts

flower stalk (stem)

leaf blade

leaf base (rolled around srem)

adventitious roots

anther   stigma

filament

one floret
(partly dissected)
– simplified view

lower scale leaf (lemma)

upper scale leaf enclosing floret (palea)

ovary

floral diagram

upper bract

palea

lemma

lateral stem to which florets are attached

stamen

stigma and style

ovary

junction of leaf blade to leaf base

ligule (membranous flap at junction, characteristic of grasses)

leaf blade

base of outer leaf

stem

base of inner leaf

stem in TS with leaf bases

Formation of pollen grains

The stamens, the male parts of flowers, consist of anther and stalk (filament). Within the anther are four long pollen sacs, and each sac consists of a central mass of diploid **pollen mother cells** surrounded by **nutritive cells** (Figure 4.7). The mother cells undergo meiosis and cell divisions, forming groups of four haploid pollen grain cells (**tetrads**). Then the tetrad breaks down as the individual **pollen grains** develop a characteristic tough, resistant outer layer to their walls (**exine**). This provides some protection from environmental dangers that may be experienced during subsequent release and transit. Finally, the pollen cell nucleus divides into a **tube nucleus** and a **generative nucleus** (Figure 4.8), of which more later. The shape and sculpturing of the outer surface of a pollen grain is specific to the species (genetically controlled), so pollen found on an insect or obtained from the air (or found in peat) can be examined microscopically and identified.

3 The exine apparently protects the contents of the pollen grain. From what dangers may it protect?

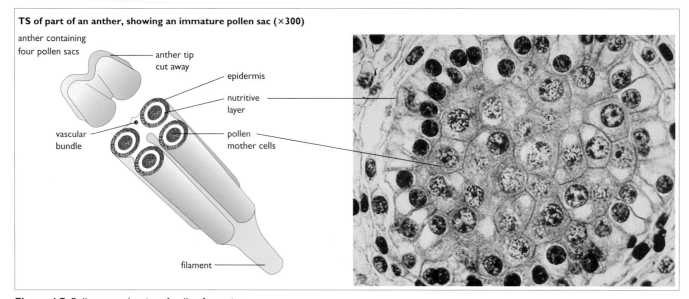

TS of part of an anther, showing an immature pollen sac (×300)

anther containing four pollen sacs

anther tip cut away

epidermis

nutritive layer

vascular bundle

pollen mother cells

filament

Figure 4.7 Pollen sacs, the site of pollen formation.

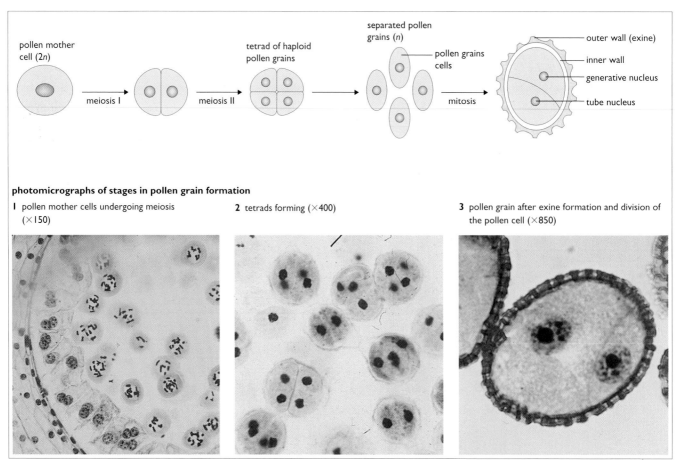

pollen mother cell (2n)

meiosis I

meiosis II

tetrad of haploid pollen grains

separated pollen grains (n)

pollen grains cells

mitosis

outer wall (exine)

inner wall

generative nucleus

tube nucleus

photomicrographs of stages in pollen grain formation

1 pollen mother cells undergoing meiosis (×150)

2 tetrads forming (×400)

3 pollen grain after exine formation and division of the pollen cell (×850)

Figure 4.8 Steps to pollen grain formation.

Release of pollen grains

In the walls of the mature anther are longitudinal rows of fibrous cells, formed between the sacs on both sides. As the walls of these cells dry, splits form along the length of the anthers, exposing the contents of the pollen sacs (Figure 4.9). Pollen grains are then free to be blown or carried away.

Figure 4.9 Release from the ripe anther.

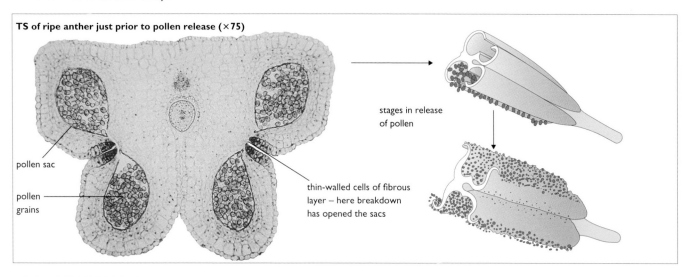

TS of ripe anther just prior to pollen release (×75)

pollen sac

pollen grains

thin-walled cells of fibrous layer – here breakdown has opened the sacs

stages in release of pollen

Extension: pollen grains and allergic reactions

Within the connective tissue of our nasal passages are many **mast cells**. These are packed with granules of heparin (a blood anticoagulant) and histamine (a chemical messenger of the body that dilates arterioles and capillaries and makes them leak plasma, and which increases mucus production). Mast cells are part of our defences against foreign matter.

The chemical composition of pollen grain walls is complex. For example, the pollen of some wind-pollinated species carry chemicals that act as antigens, binding to mast cell receptors and causing the release of histamine from the granules. The result is an attack of **hay fever**, as liquid from the blood plasma collects locally, causing swelling, and excess mucus is formed. We feel stuffed up as our breathing is hindered. Hay fever can be relieved by antihistamine preparations.

Extension: studying the past by pollen analysis

Tough though the exine is, most pollen grains are relatively short-lived. However, pollen that falls into deep water is likely to be mechanically and chemically protected in the motionless and anaerobic environment there. With the passage of geological time, pollen may be preserved if these conditions are maintained – as they are in peat, for example. In the beds of lakes that date back to the end of the last ice age (about 12 000 years ago), undisturbed peat deposits have been found. Analysis of the pollen present has revealed the dominant plant species of earlier times (Figure 4.10).

Figure 4.10 Pollen analysis of Hockham Mere, establishing dominant woodland species in past times.

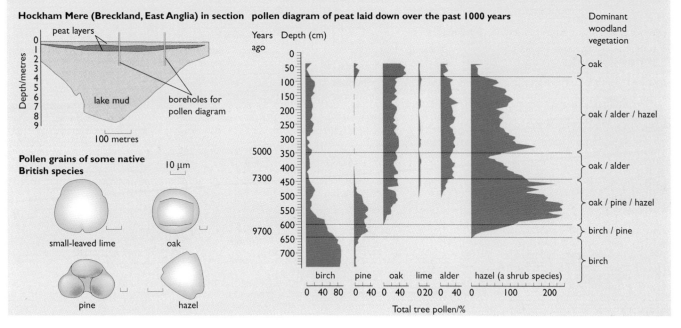

Hockham Mere (Breckland, East Anglia) in section

pollen diagram of peat laid down over the past 1000 years

Dominant woodland vegetation

peat layers

lake mud

boreholes for pollen diagram

100 metres

Pollen grains of some native British species

10 μm

small-leaved lime

oak

pine

hazel

Years ago   Depth (cm)

oak

oak / alder / hazel

oak / alder

oak / pine / hazel

birch / pine

birch

birch   pine   oak   lime   alder   hazel (a shrub species)

Total tree pollen/%

Formation of the embryo sac

The egg cell (female gamete) forms inside the embryo sac, within an ovule, inside the ovary of a flower. The sequence of nuclear and cell divisions by which the embryo sac mother cell forms a single embryo sac, and then comes to contain the **endosperm nucleus** (diploid) and **egg cell** (haploid), together with other cells (antipodals and synergids), is shown in Figure 4.11. The significance of these complex events is discussed on pages 44–45.

Figure 4.11 Formation of the embryo sac and egg cell.

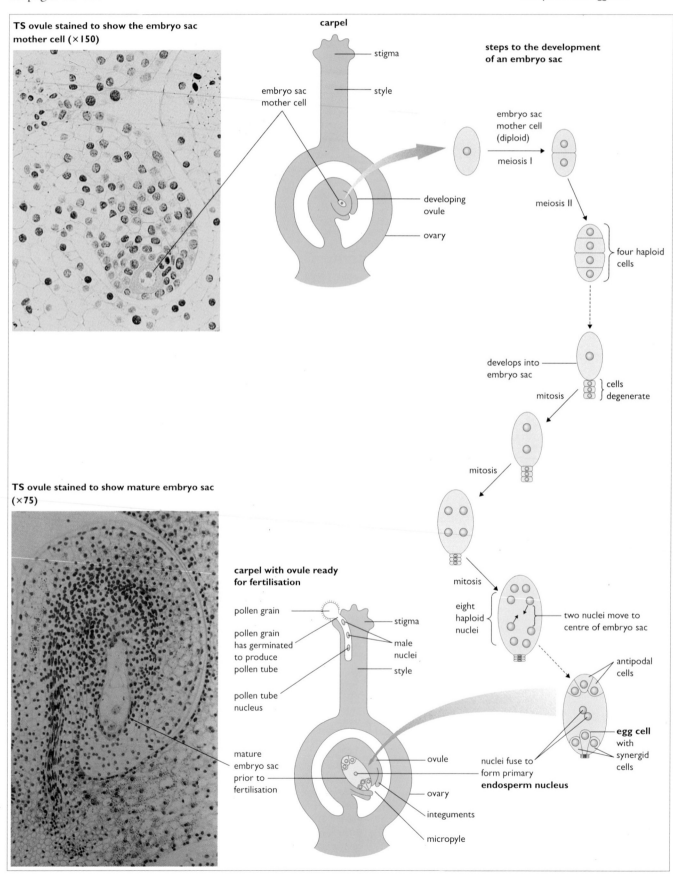

Pollination

Pollination is the transfer of pollen from a mature anther to a receptive stigma of a flower of the same species. Pollination is mostly brought about by insects or wind (Figure 4.12), but in certain species of flowering plant, water, birds or bats may be responsible. If the pollen comes from anthers in the same flower, or another flower of the same plant, this is **self-pollination**. If the pollen comes from a flower on a different plant, this is **cross-pollination**.

Figure 4.12 Pollination, and the features of insect- and wind-pollinated flowers.

---

differences between insect- and wind-pollinated flowers

Centaurea nigra (knapweed) with a marble white butterfly (*Melanargia galathea*)

Dactylis glomerata (cocksfoot grass)

insect-pollinated flowers, e.g. buttercup

- flowers in conspicuous positions
- insects attracted by colour of conspicuous petals or by scent, or both, and carry pollen from flower to flower
- nectaries secrete nectar
- stamens enclosed in flower
- pollen variable in size, with sculptured exine
- stigma small and in a position to make contact with visiting insects

wind-pollinated flowers, e.g. grass

- flowers may be produced before leaves
- air currents carry pollen, some of which may reach a flower of same species
- nectaries not present
- stamens hang outside flower
- large quantities of light, smooth pollen
- stigma large and feathery, and hanging outside flower

Mechanisms favouring cross-pollination

Mechanisms favouring cross-pollination (Figure 4.13) are common in flowering plants. Cross-pollination involves the gametes (sex cells) of two individuals, so there is greater genetic variation in the progeny than results from self-fertilisation.

4 How does genetic variation arise in progeny formed by self-fertilisation?

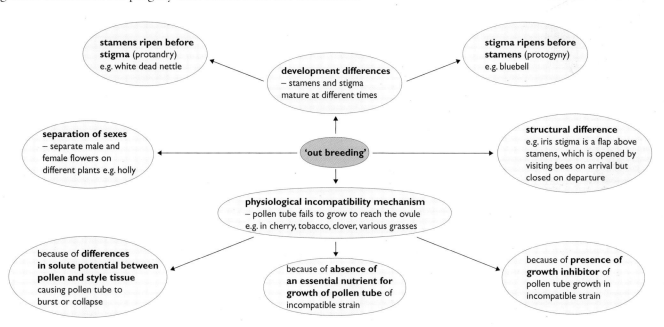

Figure 4.13 Mechanisms favouring cross-pollination.

Fertilisation

Prior to fertilisation (Figure 4.14), the generative nucleus of the pollen grain divides to form **two male nuclei** (gametes). Then, as the pollen tube grows down the style to an ovule and into the embryo sac, the male nuclei follow and enter. One nucleus fuses with the egg cell, forming a zygote; the other fuses with the (diploid) primary endosperm nucleus. This **double fertilisation** is an event unique to flowering plants.

Figure 4.14 Fertilisation.

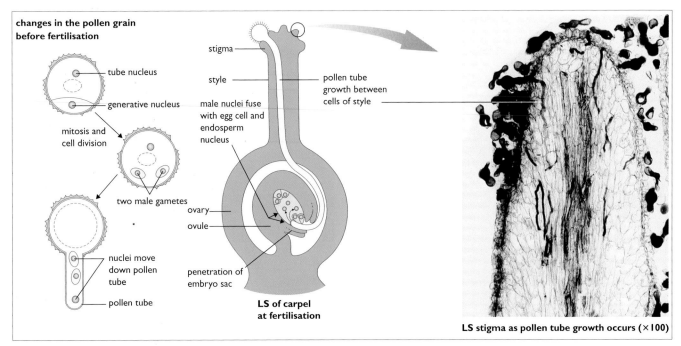

LS stigma as pollen tube growth occurs (×100)

Seed formation

The zygote divides to form a row of cells, the innermost of which forms the embryo. An embryo consists of a developing root (radicle), stem (plumule), and seed leaf or leaves (cotyledons). Simultaneously, the endosperm nucleus divides repeatedly to develop the food reserves of the seed (Figure 4.15). This double fertilisation ensures that food reserves are formed only in fertilised seeds – wasteful investments are avoided.

In summary, the seed develops from a fertilised ovule and contains an embryonic plant and food store. The fruit develops from the ovary and contains a seed or seeds.

5 Distinguish between pollination and fertilisation in flowering plants.

Figure 4.15 Steps to seed formation.

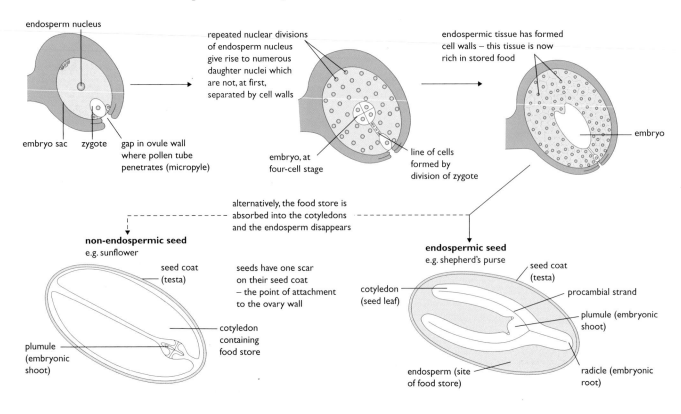

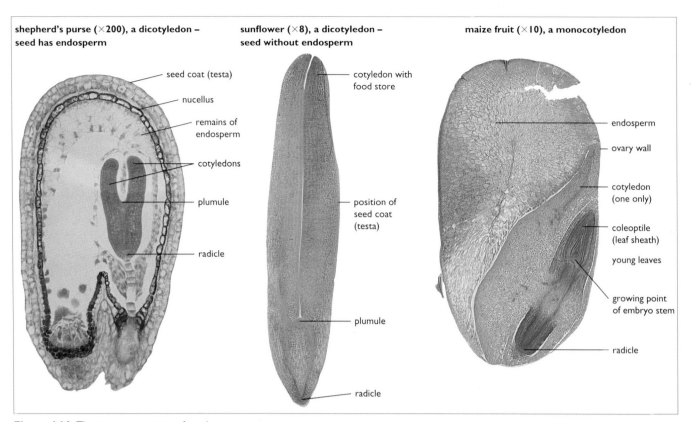

shepherd's purse (×200), a dicotyledon – seed has endosperm

- seed coat (testa)
- nucellus
- remains of endosperm
- cotyledons
- plumule
- radicle

sunflower (×8), a dicotyledon – seed without endosperm

- cotyledon with food store
- position of seed coat (testa)
- plumule
- radicle

maize fruit (×10), a monocotyledon

- endosperm
- ovary wall
- cotyledon (one only)
- coleoptile (leaf sheath)
- young leaves
- growing point of embryo stem
- radicle

Figure 4.16 The mature structure of seeds.

Extension: seed dispersal

The seed is a form in which plants may survive the unfavourable season. On formation, seeds are dormant, and may remain so until some environmental conditions trigger germination (page 67). But seeds are also the form in which plants may be dispersed, and various structures of fruits and seeds favour their being carried away from the parent plant (Figure 4.17).

Figure 4.17 Mechanisms of fruit and seed dispersal.

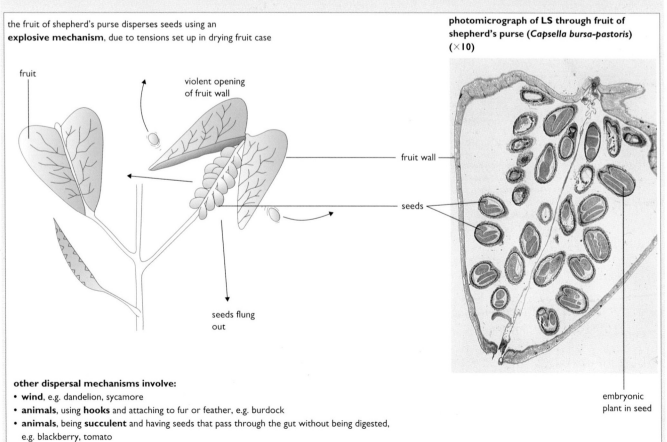

the fruit of shepherd's purse disperses seeds using an **explosive mechanism**, due to tensions set up in drying fruit case

- fruit
- violent opening of fruit wall
- seeds flung out

photomicrograph of LS through fruit of shepherd's purse (*Capsella bursa-pastoris*) (×10)

- fruit wall
- seeds
- embryonic plant in seed

other dispersal mechanisms involve:

- **wind**, e.g. dandelion, sycamore
- **animals**, using **hooks** and attaching to fur or feather, e.g. burdock
- **animals**, being **succulent** and having seeds that pass through the gut without being digested, e.g. blackberry, tomato

Extension: life cycles of green plants

The life cycle of green plants is unusual – quite different from mammals, for example. Green plants have two distinct stages, called **generations**, that alternate (Figure 4.18). These are:

- a plant built from haploid cells, which eventually produces the gametes (sex cells), called the **gametophyte generation** (the gamete-producing plant)
- a plant built from diploid cells, which eventually produces and releases spores, called the **sporophyte generation** (the spore-producing plant).

Life cycles of mosses and ferns

We can see **alternation of generation** in the life cycles of mosses (and liverworts) and ferns (Figure 4.19). However, in comparing these cycles, significant differences emerge:

- in the moss, the gametophyte is the dominant phase in the life cycle, and the sporophyte grows 'parasitically' on the gametophyte
- in the fern, the sporophyte is the dominant phase, but the gametophyte is also an independent plant (although tiny in comparison to the sporophyte).

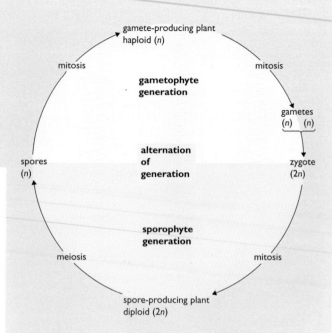

Figure 4.18 The generalised life cycle of green plants.

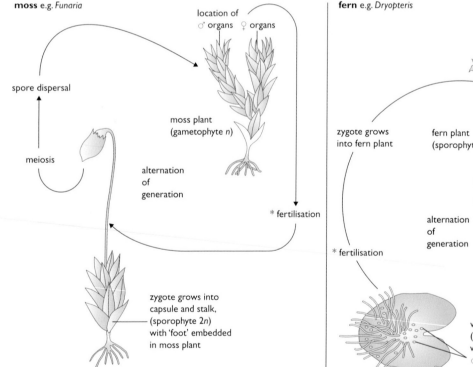
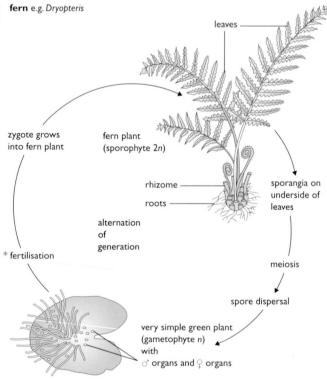

* in both mosses and ferns, the male gamete is a small, motile cell that swims in a surface film of water to the female sex cell – **both plants are dependent on moist conditions at this stage in the life cycle**

Figure 4.19 The life cycles of a moss and a fern.

Life cycle of the flowering plant

Botanists believe that the flowering plants **share common ancestors** with mosses and ferns (and conifers) – but have not evolved from them. The flowering plant life cycle provides evidence for this (Figure 4.20). It fits the alternation of generation pattern, in that:

- the flowering plant is a sporophyte plant that produces two types of spore, the microspores (pollen grains) and the megaspore (embryo sac)
- the gametophyte stage is reduced to a few redundant nuclei or cells – the pollen tube and tube nucleus are all that remain of the male gametophyte, and the antipodal and synergid cells and endosperm nucleus are what remain of the female gametophyte.

6 How does the life cycle of a mammal differ from that of the flowering plant?

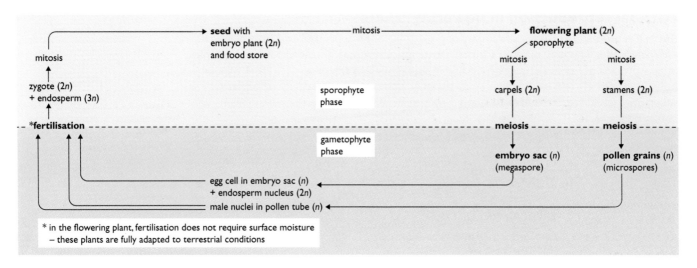

* in the flowering plant, fertilisation does not require surface moisture
  – these plants are fully adapted to terrestrial conditions

Figure 4.20 The flowering plant life cycle.

Success of the flowering plants

Flowering plants originated in the lower Cretaceous (about 150 million years ago) and rapidly became the dominant group of land plants (Figure 4.21). The success of flowering plants may be due to their:

- relatively rapid sexual reproduction – at most, it takes only weeks to form and disperse flowering plant seeds, compared to a year or more in conifers
- closed ovary, which requires the pollen tube to grow through the style before fertilisation can occur – this makes possible devices to prevent self-pollination, and thereby increases genetic variation in the progeny
- double fertilisation, so that food reserves for export are laid down only where an egg cell is also fertilised and viable seeds are formed
- efficient biochemistry, resulting in many different storage products, pigments and defence chemicals that may provide selective advantages in the colonisation of new habitats
- soft, fleshy leaves that decay rapidly after falling to the ground, allowing quick release of mineral nutrients for re-use, compared to the slow decay of conifer needles
- flowers' evolution being closely bound up with the evolution of social insects (particularly the bees), allowing efficient cross-pollination mechanisms.

7 What is the significance of meiosis in the life cycle of flowering plants?

Figure 4.21 An evolutionary diagram of land plants. Flowering plants evolved recently (they have a relatively short fossil record), but they have dominated habitats and are numerically the most common green plants.

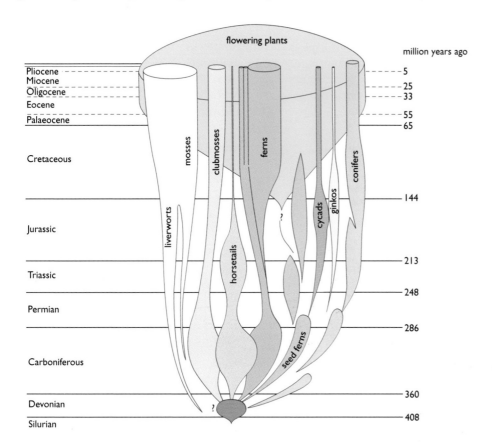

Asexual reproduction in flowering plants

Asexual reproduction occurs when part of a plant becomes separated and grows independently. The new plant(s) formed are genetically identical to the parent. Examples of this process occur in the growth cycles of organs such as rhizomes (Figure 4.22), or bulbs (e.g. onion) and stem tubers (e.g. potato). The new plants, when cut off, are substantial structures, well able to survive and grow, albeit close by the parent plant (so competing with it).

Figure 4.22 Examples of asexual reproduction in flowering plants.

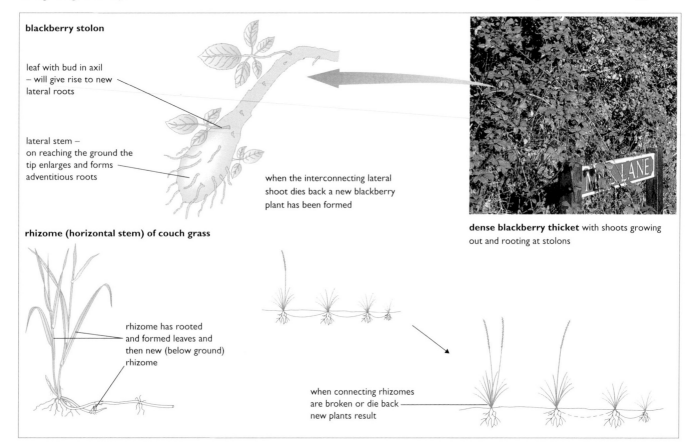

Commercial propagation of flowering plants

The potential for asexual reproduction in flowering plants is exploited commercially in the vegetative propagation by growers of plants (such as flowers, vegetables and shrubs) for sale in garden centres (Figure 4.23). The products, being clones of the parent plant, show the desired characteristics of the parent plant. A **clone** is a group of genetically identical cells or individuals, all derived from an individual by repeated asexual divisions.

8 Why are clones potentially useful to commercial botanists?

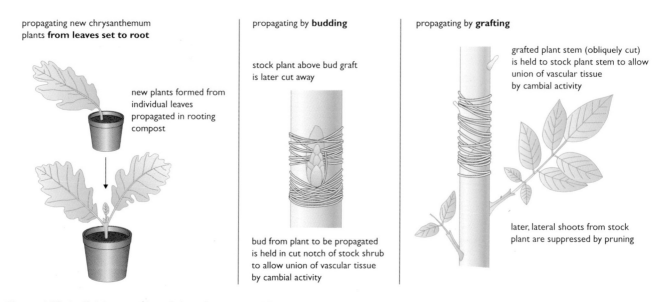

Figure 4.23 Artificial propagation of plants for commercial purposes.

Plant tissue culture

Plant tissue culture (Figure 4.24) is a laboratory technique for growing new plants from blocks of undifferentiated tissue (such as callus), or even from individual cells. Unlimited numbers of clones of a plant can be produced, all identical. By this technique, genetically modified cells can also be cloned and grown up into plants. So the techniques of tissue culture have increasingly important applications in agriculture, horticulture and genetic engineering.

Figure 4.24 The techniques of tissue culture applied to flowering plants.

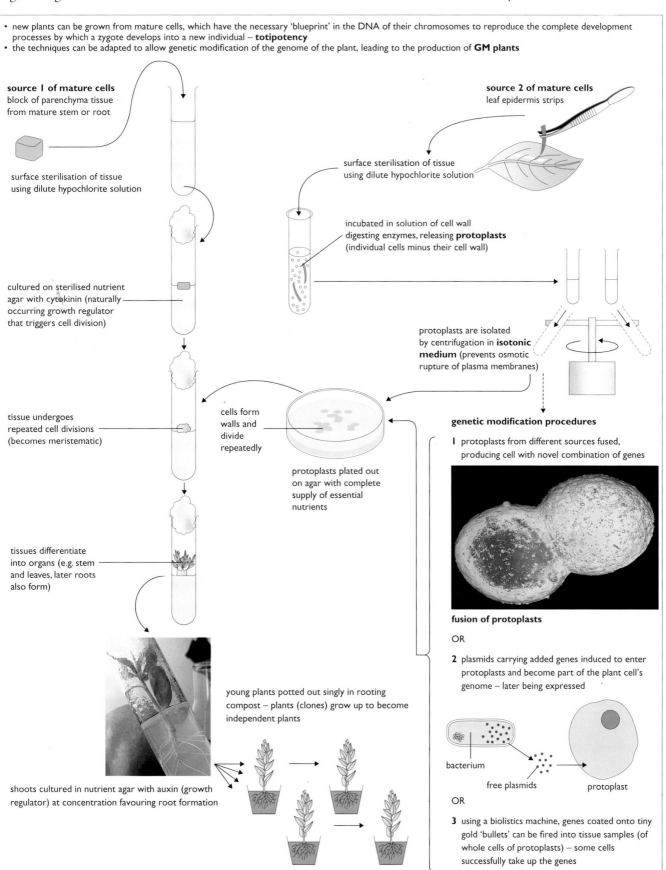

- new plants can be grown from mature cells, which have the necessary 'blueprint' in the DNA of their chromosomes to reproduce the complete development processes by which a zygote develops into a new individual – **totipotency**
- the techniques can be adapted to allow genetic modification of the genome of the plant, leading to the production of **GM plants**

source 1 of mature cells
block of parenchyma tissue from mature stem or root

surface sterilisation of tissue using dilute hypochlorite solution

cultured on sterilised nutrient agar with cytokinin (naturally occurring growth regulator that triggers cell division)

tissue undergoes repeated cell divisions (becomes meristematic)

tissues differentiate into organs (e.g. stem and leaves, later roots also form)

shoots cultured in nutrient agar with auxin (growth regulator) at concentration favouring root formation

young plants potted out singly in rooting compost – plants (clones) grow up to become independent plants

source 2 of mature cells
leaf epidermis strips

surface sterilisation of tissue using dilute hypochlorite solution

incubated in solution of cell wall digesting enzymes, releasing **protoplasts** (individual cells minus their cell wall)

protoplasts are isolated by centrifugation in **isotonic medium** (prevents osmotic rupture of plasma membranes)

cells form walls and divide repeatedly

protoplasts plated out on agar with complete supply of essential nutrients

genetic modification procedures

1 protoplasts from different sources fused, producing cell with novel combination of genes

fusion of protoplasts

OR

2 plasmids carrying added genes induced to enter protoplasts and become part of the plant cell's genome – later being expressed

bacterium

free plasmids

protoplast

OR

3 using a biolistics machine, genes coated onto tiny gold 'bullets' can be fired into tissue samples (of whole cells of protoplasts) – some cells successfully take up the genes

Genetic modification of commercial crops

Plants (and animals) used in agriculture and horticulture have been obtained by genetic manipulation of wild organisms. There are two ways this is done.

Artificial selection

In traditional breeding projects, the most useful offspring for a particular purpose are selected and used as the next generation of parents. Offspring regarded as less useful are prevented from breeding. The effect of repeating this artificial selection process, generation after generation, is relative speedy – deliberate genetic change, sometimes leading to new varieties of organisms. This technique has been applied with increasing sophistication since Neolithic times, and is still in common use by researchers and horticulturalists, for example.

Genetic engineering (recombinant DNA technology)

Today, genetic modification (GM) is also achieved by the direct transfer of genes from one organism to the set of genes (**genome**) of another, often **unrelated** organism. In green plants, introducing genes into cells is complicated by the presence of the cell wall. However, cell walls may be temporarily removed by the gentle action of enzymes, leaving cell protoplasts. Genes may be introduced into a protoplast, or different protoplasts may be induced to fuse, rather like gametes do (Figure 4.24, page 47). Alternatively, genetic modification can be brought about by the tumour-forming bacterium *Agrobacterium*. The gene for tumour formation occurs in a plasmid. Useful genes may also be added to the plasmid – then the gall tissue that the bacterium induces in a plant it attacks (and the new plants grown from it) may contain and express the new gene (these techniques are outlined in *Illustrated Advanced Biology: Genetics and Evolution*, this series, page 52). Examples of GM plants are illustrated in Figures 4.25 and 4.26. Genetically modified plants are available or are being developed as major commercial products (Figure 4.27). The rate at which these are used in the UK and new ones are developed depends largely on public reactions to this little understood technology (Table 4.2).

9 What are plasmids and where do they naturally occur?

oilseed rape (*Brassica napus*) flowering in March/April

oilseed rape

- the fourth most widely grown crop in the UK
- about 500 000 ha cultivated, yielding 3.5 t/ha
- two forms are grown
  - *Brassica napus*, 'winter rape', sown late August/September, harvested in the following July
  - *Brassica rapa*, 'spring rape', sown late March/ early April, harvested August/September

harvested seeds

yield oils for margarine and cooking, and protein meal for animal feeds (a variety with erucic acid is the source of erucamide, a 'slip agent' in polythene manufacture)

how oilseed rapes are being genetically modified

- GM rape has been produced that is tolerant of the non-selective herbicide **glufosinate** (which kills surrounding weeds) – rape is a poor competitor with weeds for soil nitrates
- additional GM oilseed rape varieties are in preparation that have increased resistance to pests or that supply different oils/fatty acids for use in detergents, paints, polymers, pharmaceuticals, inks, lubricants and cosmetics

harvesting of oilseed rape seeds is by combine harvester

Figure 4.25 Genetic modification of oilseed rape.

Figure 4.26 Genetic engineering in forestry – eco-friendly paper production.

poplar trees, one of the hardwood species used for paper manufacture

pulp obtained from softwoods, e.g. spruce; hardwoods, e.g. poplar

pulp production process

woods contain 15–25% lignin

bark removed → wood cut into chips → *****extraction of fibres** and lignin removal by chemical treatment e.g. alkaline sulphate (NaOH + Na$_2$SO$_2$) → *****bleaching of fibre pulp** using chlorine, hydrogen peroxide or sulphur dioxide

paper making from pulp → roughening of fibres → chemical additions to form papers of differing properties → pulp slurry formed into paper film on moving mesh → water squeezed out by rollers

self-supporting paper dried

additional treatments → surface sized to waterproof / surface coated with clay and latex binder (for quality printing) → surface smoothed and polished → stored on roller, cut to size

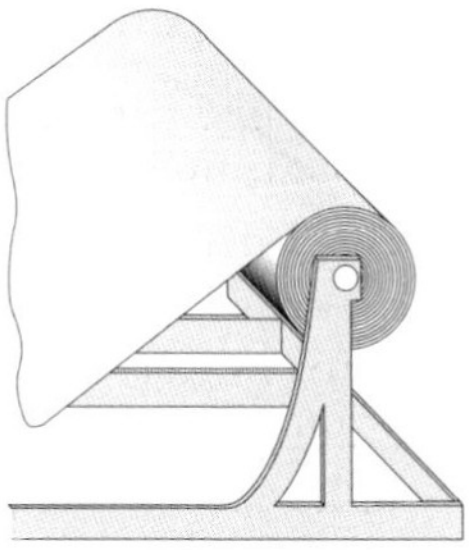

aspen trees (*Populus tremuloides*) have been produced that are genetically modified to contain 45% less lignin:

- less energy and fewer toxic chemicals are required to extract the fibres
- less bleach is used and more paper pulp is produced
- trees grow faster
- male and female flowers are on separate plants – only female trees have been genetically engineered in this programme

*****paper mills have a high environmental impact** due to the harmful effects of the chemicals that degrade lignin and bleach the pulp – also, large quantities of water are required in paper-making

Table 4.2 Evaluating GM crops – possible advantages and hazards

Advantages	Hazards
Photosynthetically enhanced varieties, e.g. by introducing genes for C$_4$ photosynthesis (page 54) into C$_3$ plants, such as rice and potato, thereby increasing yields	Contravention of a principle that humans should not tamper with nature in any way
Resistance to virus attack in crops, e.g. in maize, cucumber, melon, potato, tomato	GM technology is highly expensive and the funds invested could be diverted to have greater beneficial effects for more people if fundamental problems of diet and living conditions were tackled by traditional methods instead
Resistance to insect damage in crops, e.g. apple, oilseed rape, maize, cotton, rice, strawberry, tomato	Addition of novel or 'foreign' genes to a genome might cause the recipient organism to function in an unforeseen way, harmful to surrounding organisms
Improved ripening characteristics in marketed fruit, reducing amount of crop losses post-harvest, e.g. tomato	Herbicide-resistant crops allow blanket application of very powerful herbicides in quantities and ways harmful to the surrounding flora (and fauna – including soil microorganisms)
Change in composition of stored fats and oils in seeds, making available chemicals previously obtained via industrial manufacturing processes, e.g. oilseed rape	Farmers who use herbicide-resistant crops have to purchase the specific herbicide involved, losing the ability to 'shop around' for competitive prices, and so increasing their dependence on a single multinational supplier
Introduction of essential vitamins into plant products otherwise deficient in this vitamin (e.g. β-carotene, vitamin A into rice grains) – rice is the staple of about 60% of the human population, many of whom are unable to afford vitamin supplements	Genes for herbicide tolerance can pass from crop plants (e.g. oilseed rape) to related hedgerow species (e.g. wild turnip, wild radish) to produce 'superweeds' (which have a selective advantage over other wild plants if the plants of the hedgerow are also sprayed with the weedkiller)
Production of vaccines for human (or animal) immunity to diseases (e.g. HIV, foot-and-mouth disease) – production takes place in plants, using plant viruses as vectors	
Production of eco-friendly wood (reduced lignin content) for pulp for paper production	
Herbicide tolerance in crop plants, e.g. oilseed rape, maize, cotton, potato, soybean, tomato	

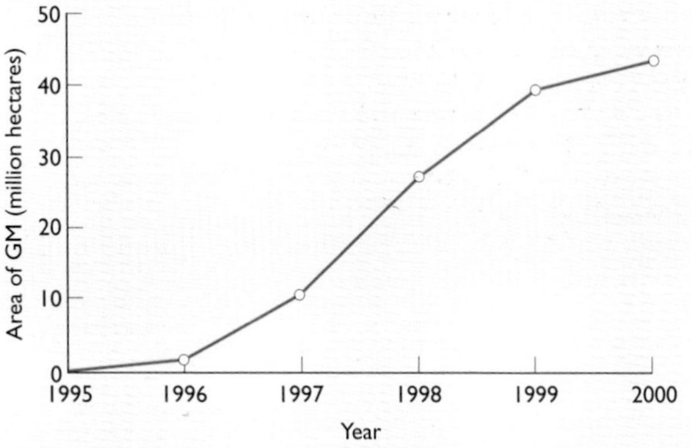

Figure 4.27 Global area of GM crops, 1996–2000.

5 Plants that feed and serve us

We use plants not only as foods, but also as raw materials for industries such as forestry, medicine, fabric and clothing manufacture, dyeing, and many other industrial, scientific and technical uses. These are summarised in Figure 5.1, where the divisions are comparative, based on the numbers of most commonly exploited species. However, there is no reference here to the huge numbers of decorative plants used in gardens and parklands, nor to the vast, worldwide uses of plant matter as fuel.

Plants in our diet

Plant material of different botanical origins (stem, leaf, root, bud, fruit, seed, inflorescence) are used as food, sometimes as vegetables and sometimes as fruits (Figure 5.2).

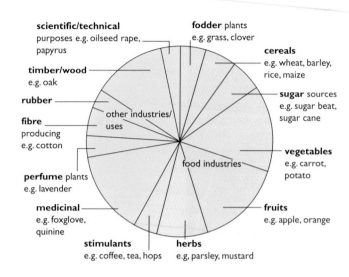

Figure 5.1 (above) How we use plants.

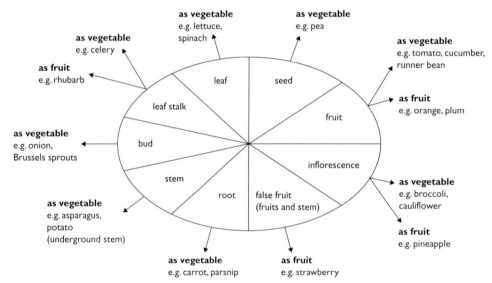

Figure 5.2 (left) The botanical origins of the plant matter in our diet.

Importance of the grass family

Plant matter forms the bulk of human food intake in both developed and less-developed countries, but it is plants of one family – the grasses – that we, and most of our livestock, depend on (Figure 5.3). Cereals are relatively easy to grow, and the mature grains they yield are comparatively easily stored. Grains contain significant quantities of protein as well as starch. Cows and sheep (and all other ruminants) feed mostly on grass leaves, rather than necessarily requiring precious grain stocks.

1 Why does grain fed to humans sustain many more people than when fed to livestock for meat production for human consumption?

Figure 5.3 Plant matter as a proportion of the human diet – and the significance of grasses.

Bangladesh
population >133 000 000
plant matter in diets = 96%
(cereals = 82.1%)

% of diet from cereals
(cultivated grasses)

UK
population >59 000 000
plant matter in diets = 63%
(cereals = 21%)

% of diet from other plant matter

% of diet from animal matter

Grasslands

Grasslands occur naturally, as prairies and savannahs, and also as a cultivated crop (Figure 5.4). In temperate climates, grasses grow vigorously in the spring, and again after flowering. Wherever they grow, their extensive fibrous root system is highly effective in combating soil erosion. Grass leaves are cropped by grazing ruminant herbivores, whether wild animals or maintained herds of sheep and cows. Because the grass plant has growing points at each node (**intercalary meristems** rather than a single apical meristem – see Figure 2.10, page 8), growth of grass continues, unharmed, when the tips of shoots are cropped (Figure 5.5).

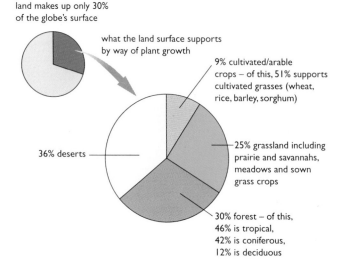

land makes up only 30% of the globe's surface

what the land surface supports by way of plant growth

9% cultivated/arable crops – of this, 51% supports cultivated grasses (wheat, rice, barley, sorghum)

36% deserts

25% grassland including prairie and savannahs, meadows and sown grass crops

30% forest – of this, 46% is tropical, 42% is coniferous, 12% is deciduous

Figure 5.5 (below) Growth of grass as a crop.

Figure 5.4 (above right) The importance of grassland, worldwide.

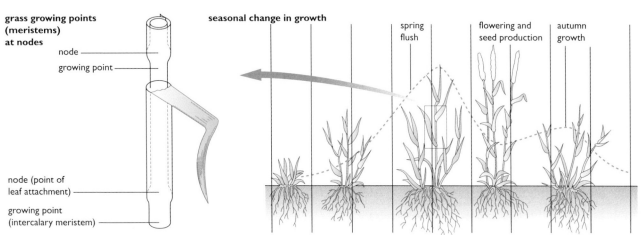

grass growing points (meristems) at nodes

node

growing point

node (point of leaf attachment)

growing point (intercalary meristem)

seasonal change in growth

spring flush

flowering and seed production

autumn growth

Hay and silage production

Excess summer grass may be preserved by the farmer for winter use.

For **hay** (Figure 5.6), the cut grass is dried naturally in the field, reducing the moisture content from 90% or more, in fresh grass, to below 20% before baling and storage. Hay should be cut well before flowering stems grow up and leaf proteins start to be transferred to the seeds (see Figure 5.9, page 53). Good hay smells sweet (not musty) and consists of dried leaves. Excess handling of hay (e.g. in delayed drying) may reduce dry leaves to powder, which is then lost to the stock being fed.

For **silage** (Figure 5.7), grass is cut and briefly wilted (water content reduced to about 65–75%) before being transported to a silage barn or pit, and compressed to exclude excess air, or baled in large plastic bags. In both, the rapid exclusion of air suppresses growth of yeasts, moulds and bacteria that form compost. Instead, anaerobic conditions cause fermentation bacteria to attack the moist organic matter and produce organic acids. The pH falls to about 4.8–4.0, and causes the food value of the fermented grass to be maintained. Good silage is yellow-green, smells acidic, and is rich in leafy matter.

2 Grass crops grown for silage are often planted with clover or lucerne (leguminous plants). How does this improve the value of the silage?

Figure 5.6 Hay making.

Figure 5.7 Silage making.

Cultivated grasses as sources of grain

The cereals

Wheat, barley and **oats** are the most important arable crops in the UK. They are examples of **mesophytes** – plants adapted to temperate climates with normal amounts of rainfall. For example, wheat grows best in cool springs with moderate moisture for early growth, followed by sunny summer months that turn dry, for harvesting. Bread wheat (*Triticum aestivum*, Figure 5.8) is a hexaploid ($2n = 42$), and arose by natural crossings of various wild wheats ($2n = 14$) that occurred in the Fertile Crescent of the Middle East about 8000 years ago. Today, **'winter' wheat** varieties are planted in the autumn, and they root and tiller (produce side shoots at ground level) before the low temperatures of winter suspend growth. The crop matures in early summer. **'Spring' wheats** are sown after winter, and are adapted to a shorter growing season (but give lighter yields). There are two classes of wheat variety. **Hard wheats** are higher in proteins, are grown in areas of lower rainfall, and are used to produce bread that keeps. **Soft wheat** varieties are more starchy, are used to make French bread and pasta, and are grown in more humid conditions.

Figure 5.8 The structure of wheat.

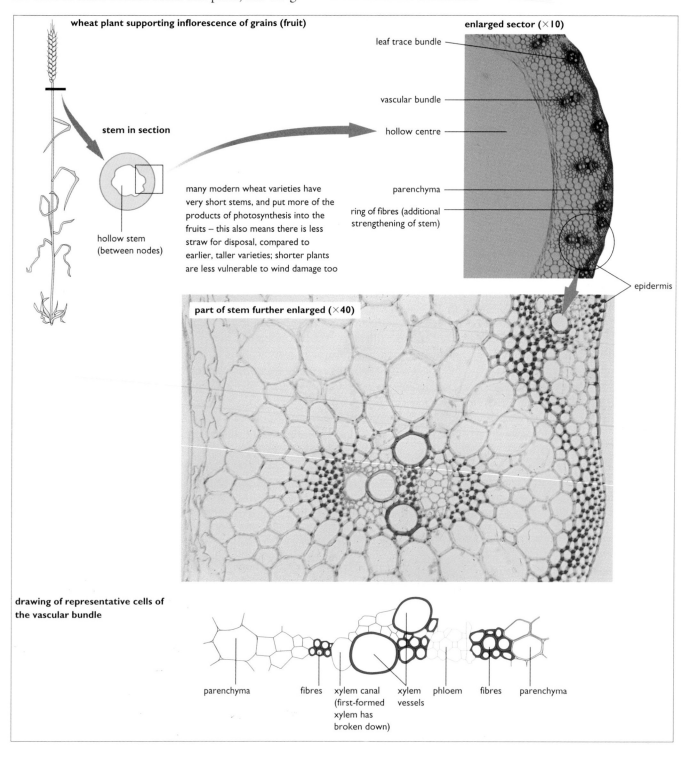

Growth and metabolism of the developing wheat plant

Wheat plants, once established, develop **tillers** (additional stems formed from buds at the base of the main stem). Then growth of stems and leaves occurs before the formation of the inflorescence and flowers. Finally, the grains (fruits) form. Associated with these stages are the uptake of nitrates and other ions, and the formation and mobilisation of key metabolites, particularly amino acids, around the plant (Figure 5.9).

Figure 5.9 The pattern of combined nitrogen absorption and distribution.

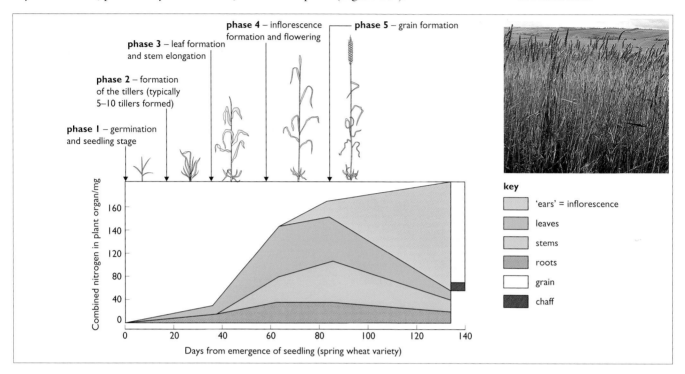

phase **1** – germination and seedling stage

phase **2** – formation of the tillers (typically 5–10 tillers formed)

phase **3** – leaf formation and stem elongation

phase **4** – inflorescence formation and flowering

phase **5** – grain formation

key
- 'ears' = inflorescence
- leaves
- stems
- roots
- grain
- chaff

Combined nitrogen in plant organ/mg

Days from emergence of seedling (spring wheat variety)

Barley and oats as crops

Barley varieties are grown for animal feed and also for malting. Oats are grown less commonly, and are used for animal feeds or for oatmeal for human consumption.

3 Examine the graph in Figure 5.9.

a) What might be the best time for the application of nitrate-based fertiliser?

b) What are the steps by which nitrate absorbed from the soil becomes built into protein?

c) How do the amino acids, produced at the root tips, reach the leaves?

d) Rubisco is the major protein in leaves. Why is this such an important component of plants?

e) How is leaf protein transported to the developing grain?

Figure 5.10 Productivity of wheat.

improved yields are due to more productive varieties (better tillering, shorter stems, more grains per inflorescence, heavier grains) and the wide-scale use of pesticides (fungicides, insecticides, molluscicides, herbicides) and the carefully targeted application of fertilisers

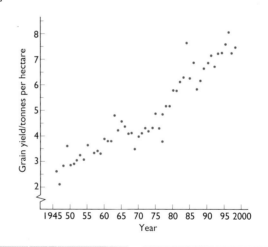

Grain yield/tonnes per hectare

Year

seed grain is sown at the rate of 150–185 kg/hectare (winter wheat) and 185–250 kg/hectare (spring wheat)

Figure 5.11 Barley.

Figure 5.12 Oats.

Maize – a C$_4$ plant

Cultivated maize (Figure 5.13) originated in southern Mexico, from wild forms, by natural crossings. The original varieties are now extinct, but maize similar to today's varieties soon spread throughout much of north and south America. It became the staple food for early humans there, as wheat did in the Old World. Maize required a relatively long season to ripen, and was strongly moisture-loving. However, as a result of selective breeding over many years, different varieties now yield a heavy crop under quite diverse conditions. In fact, modern varieties differ profoundly from the original form. Today maize survives only because of cultivation by humans. For example, the fruits do not dislodge from the cob but remain there, wrapped in husks. Natural dispersal is impossible. However, maize has been carried to all continents by humans, and grows well in favourable environments. The plant is grown widely as fodder for stock (e.g. for silage), as well as for human consumption.

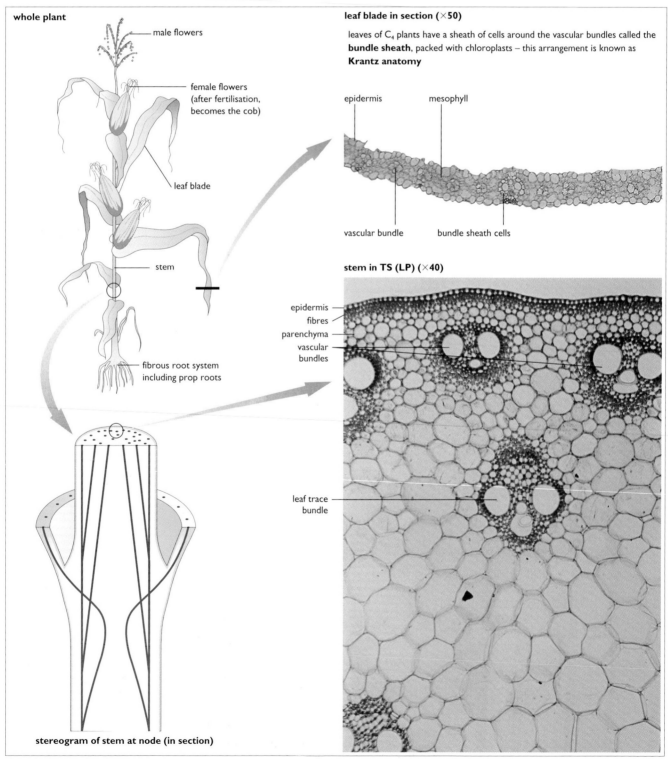

whole plant
- male flowers
- female flowers (after fertilisation, becomes the cob)
- leaf blade
- stem
- fibrous root system including prop roots

stereogram of stem at node (in section)

leaf blade in section (×50)

leaves of C$_4$ plants have a sheath of cells around the vascular bundles called the **bundle sheath**, packed with chloroplasts – this arrangement is known as **Krantz anatomy**

- epidermis
- mesophyll
- vascular bundle
- bundle sheath cells

stem in TS (LP) (×40)

- epidermis
- fibres
- parenchyma
- vascular bundles
- leaf trace bundle

Figure 5.13 The structure of maize (*Zea mays*).

Photosynthesis in C₄ plants

The fixation of CO_2 in the light-independent step of photosynthesis (Figure 3.20, page 33) in green plants of temperate climates is called the **C₃ pathway** – because the first product is a three-carbon compound. Many tropical plants also produce four-carbon compounds as initial products of photosynthesis, mainly the organic acid malate, and these are known as **C₄ plants**. In Figure 5.14 the nature of C₄ photosynthesis is shown. The value of additional C₄ fixation (as a mechanism of preventing photorespiration – see Extension, this page) is outlined in Figure 5.15.

4 In C₄ plants, CO_2 is fixed in the bundle sheath cells as well as the mesophyll cells. How does CO_2 fixation differ in these two (adjacent) locations?

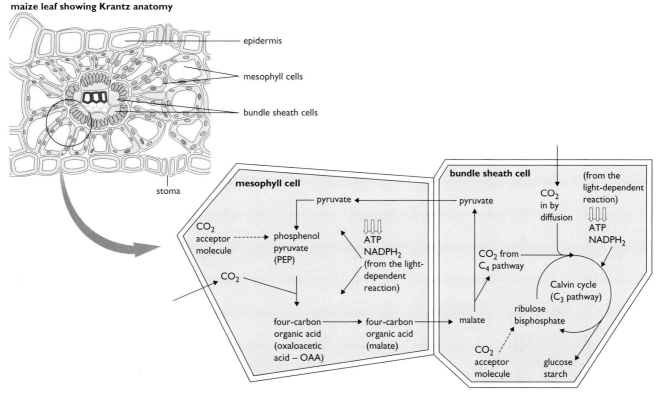

Figure 5.14 The site and steps to C₄ photosynthesis.

Extension: photorespiration

Photosynthesis evolved in an atmosphere of low oxygen concentration but high CO_2 concentration. In today's atmosphere (about 21% O_2), oxygen has become a competitive inhibitor for the active site of Rubisco, the enzyme that fixes CO_2 in photosynthesis (page 33). Inhibition by oxygen is greatest in very high sunlight (as experienced by tropical/sub-tropical plants). The result is the breakdown of the five-carbon acceptor molecule ribulose bisphosphate to a two-carbon compound (and one molecule of the normal three-carbon sugar product), thus reducing the yield from photosynthesis. So the advantage of C₄ photosynthesis is that it delivers more CO_2 to the chloroplasts, blocking out wasteful photorespiration.

Figure 5.15 Rubisco – in photosynthesis and photorespiration.

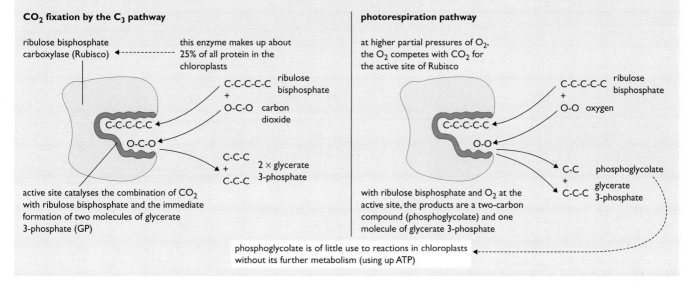

Sorghum – a grain plant adapted to arid conditions

Sorghum is a member of the grass family, a plant of hot, semi-arid tropical environments where annual rainfall is typically only 400–600 mm (habitats much too dry for maize). Sorghum has become the fifth most important world cereal, after wheat, rice, maize and barley. Like maize, it is a C_4 plant. Structural adaptations that aid survival in drought conditions are shown in the growth of its roots and the structure of its leaves (Figure 5.16).

Figure 5.16 *Sorghum bicolor* as a drought-resistant, tropical plant.

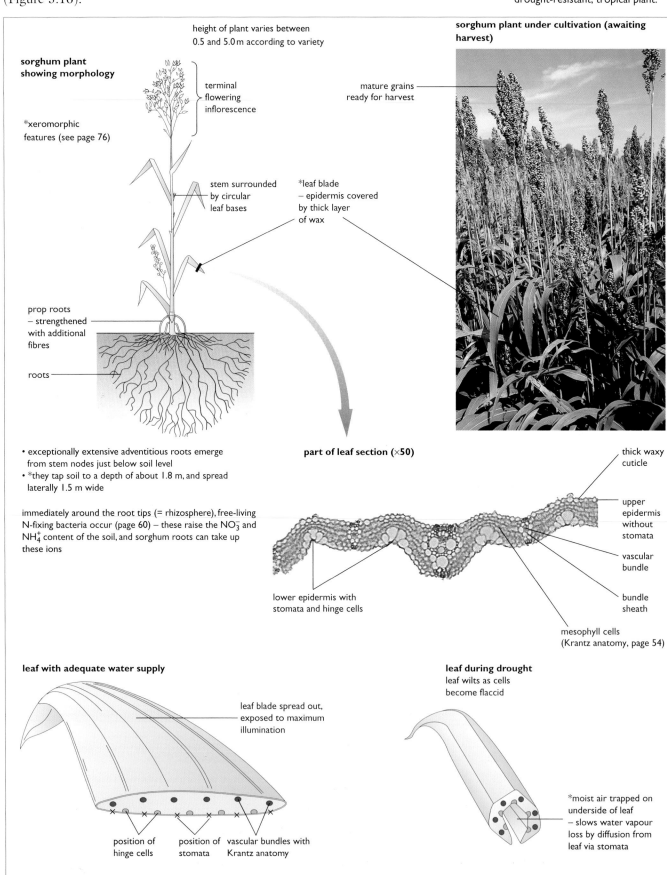

height of plant varies between 0.5 and 5.0 m according to variety

sorghum plant under cultivation (awaiting harvest)

sorghum plant showing morphology

terminal flowering inflorescence

*xeromorphic features (see page 76)

mature grains ready for harvest

stem surrounded by circular leaf bases

*leaf blade – epidermis covered by thick layer of wax

prop roots – strengthened with additional fibres

roots

• exceptionally extensive adventitious roots emerge from stem nodes just below soil level
• *they tap soil to a depth of about 1.8 m, and spread laterally 1.5 m wide

immediately around the root tips (= rhizosphere), free-living N-fixing bacteria occur (page 60) – these raise the NO_3^- and NH_4^+ content of the soil, and sorghum roots can take up these ions

part of leaf section (×50)

thick waxy cuticle

upper epidermis without stomata

vascular bundle

bundle sheath

lower epidermis with stomata and hinge cells

mesophyll cells (Krantz anatomy, page 54)

leaf with adequate water supply

leaf blade spread out, exposed to maximum illumination

position of hinge cells

position of stomata

vascular bundles with Krantz anatomy

leaf during drought
leaf wilts as cells become flaccid

*moist air trapped on underside of leaf – slows water vapour loss by diffusion from leaf via stomata

The origins and current cultivation of sorghum

Sorghum originated in central/north eastern Africa (Figure 5.17), where the greatest variability in wild species is still found. With domestication, the plant spread throughout Africa. Sorghum reached India at least 3000 years ago, and China (via the 'silk road') by the thirteenth century. Sorghum was carried to the USA during the 1800s, on slave ships from West Africa, and today most is grown there (Figure 5.18). The wide range of uses to which it is put is shown in Figure 5.19.

Figure 5.17 Origin and distribution of sorghum.

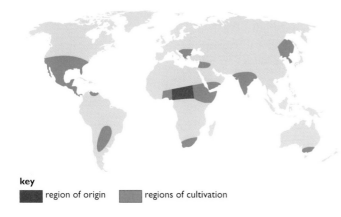

Figure 5.18 Major producers of sorghum.

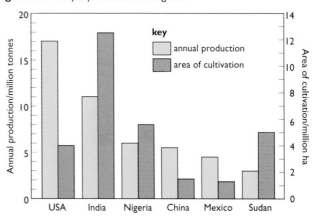

Figure 5.19 The varieties of sorghum and their different uses.

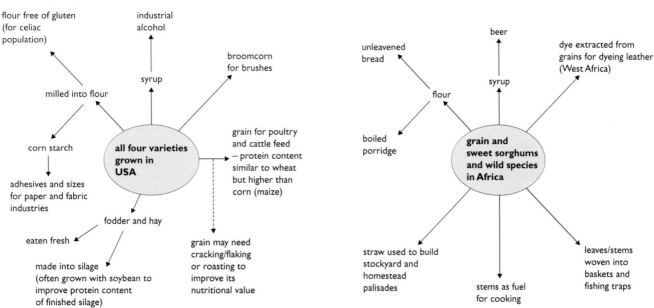

Sorghum and the global economy

In areas where sorghum has long been the traditional dietary staple, particularly in Africa, there has been an influx of grains such as wheat and maize from economically more successful regions, chiefly North America. People have found the latter grains easier to prepare and cook, and the products more palatable. Consequently, traditional agricultural production has suffered, especially where cash crops have been required to help pay for imports. But when severe droughts cause other crops to fail, local farmers have turned to sorghum as the crop that is better adapted to the climate. Successful plant breeding of sorghum (including by genetic engineering, perhaps) is urgently required to:

* combine the higher yield properties of American hybrid varieties with the resistance to pests of the African wild types
* improve qualities such as ease of husk removal and palatability of foods produced from the grains.

5 What characteristics do varieties of sorghum adapted to conditions in Africa potentially offer to the plant crop breeder?

Rice – the most important human food crop

Rice is the staple for more than 60% of the world's population (more wheat is produced than rice, but wheat is also used extensively in animal feeds). Today, rice is grown in the USA, South America and Africa, as well as in the paddy fields of Asia. The plant was domesticated in south-west Asia, probably 12 000 years ago, which is much earlier than the first records of cultivated wheat (in the Fertile Crescent). If so, rice has certainly fed more people over a longer period than any other crop.

The growth of cultivated rice

Rice (*Oryza sativa*, Asian and *O. glaberrima*, African) is a semi-aquatic annual grass that flourishes in poorly draining, silty soils. Relatively high temperatures and high rainfall are required. Consequently, rice grows well in waterlogged paddy fields in tropical regions. However, it is not strictly an aquatic plant. Some varieties grow in upland fields (as wheat is cultivated), although these give lower yields. For paddy field cultivation, seedlings are often germinated in moist soil and transplanted into flooded fields as young plants. Once established, rice plants tend to tiller (form side-shoots) extensively (Figures 5.20 and 5.22), and varieties in which the tillers eventually develop inflorescences are selected because they give higher grain yields. The growth cycle lasts between three and six months, from vegetative growth to flowering and fruit formation, according to variety and climate. Before harvest, paddy fields are usually drained. If there is sufficient water, a second crop of rice may be grown immediately, largely because of the natural fertility of the paddy field.

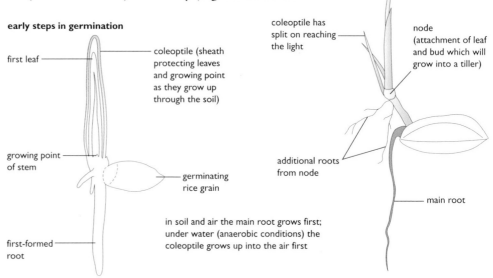

Figure 5.20 Germinating rice.

Azolla *fern,* Anabaena *and the fertilisation of paddy field soil*

Azolla, a tiny, aquatic fern, grows profusely in flooded paddy fields, for example in China and Vietnam. Living in cavities of the fern leaf is *Anabaena azollae* (Figure 5.21). This cyanobacterium is nitrogen-fixing, and the ammonium ions formed are shared with the fern cells. When the fern dies and decays, the soil of the paddy field is fertilised with additional combined nitrogen, which supports growth of the rice plants and makes possible productive, intensive cultivation of rice. Human agriculture has benefited for centuries, long before plant nutrition was understood.

6 Rice has an indirect association with *Anabaena*, a cyanobacterium. What advantage comes to rice from this relationship?

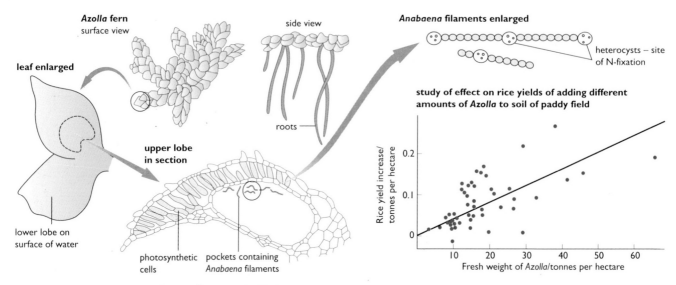

Figure 5.21 *Azolla* as a nitrogen-fixation factory for paddy field rice.

Rice growth in waterlogged soils

The presence of aerenchyma tissue (parenchyma with huge, interconnecting air spaces between the cells) in the stems and roots of rice facilitates diffusion of oxygen to root cells growing in waterlogged soil, typically 5–10 cm below the water surface.

Figure 5.22 The structure of mature rice plants, as vegetative growth gives way to fruit formation.

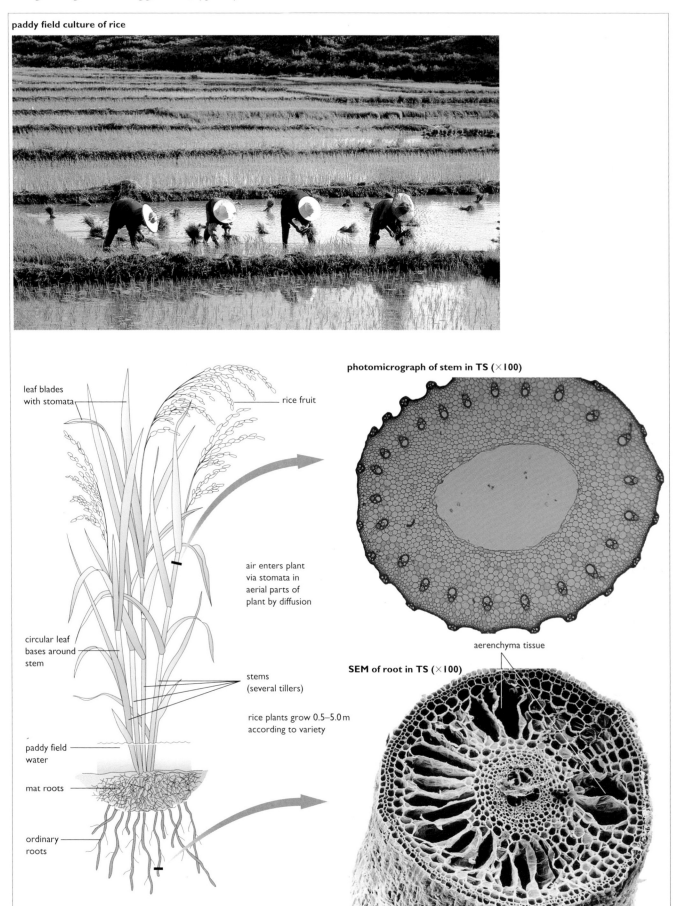

paddy field culture of rice

leaf blades with stomata

rice fruit

photomicrograph of stem in TS (×100)

air enters plant via stomata in aerial parts of plant by diffusion

circular leaf bases around stem

stems (several tillers)

rice plants grow 0.5–5.0 m according to variety

aerenchyma tissue

SEM of root in TS (×100)

paddy field water

mat roots

ordinary roots

Leguminous plants, *Rhizobium* and nitrogen fixation

Some microorganisms have the facility to fix atmospheric nitrogen, and produce combined nitrogen compounds such as ammonia and nitrates. In these forms, the element nitrogen is available to be built up into amino acids and proteins. Free-living organisms able to do this include cyanobacteria such as *Anabaena* (page 58). Other bacteria, such as *Rhizobium*, may live in mutualistic association with plant root cells. Rhizobium commonly occurs in the soil around plant roots (a region called the rhizosphere). The bacterium feeds on dead organic matter here, but is also able to enter the roots of members of the Legume family of flowering plants if they are growing nearby. The bacterium causes the host tissues to form into a nodule around the cells infected with it (Figure 5.23). Here *Rhizobium* produces the enzyme nitrogenase, and reduces nitrogen gas to ammonia using energy and reducing power obtained by respiration of sugars taken from its host plant.

$$N_2 + 8e^- + 16ATP + 16H_2O \rightarrow 2NH_3 + H_2 + 16ADP + 16P_i + 8H^+$$

The ammonia is combined with organic acids to form amino acids, and many of the amino acids pass out to the surrounding cells and are used by the host plant. Because of their association with the bacterium *Rhizobium*, leguminous plants can flourish in poor soils. Also, as crop plants rich in proteins (Table 5.1), they have additional value in agriculture and human nutrition.

7 Both *Anabaena* and *Rhizobium* 'fix' atmospheric nitrogen. What major advantage does the latter have, when housed in root nodules, that is not available to free-living N-fixing organisms?

Table 5.1 Protein content of foods

Food source	Percentage protein
Cereals	
Whole rice	7.5–9.0
Polished rice	5.2–7.5
Wheat flour	9.8–13.5
Maize meal	7.0–9.4
Legume seeds	
Phaseolus beans	25–49
Soybean	33–42
Peanut	25–30
Root crop	
Potato (dry weight)	10–13

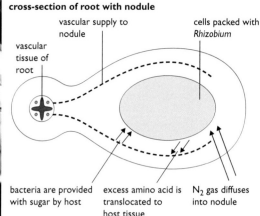

cross-section of root with nodule

vascular supply to nodule

cells packed with *Rhizobium*

vascular tissue of root

bacteria are provided with sugar by host

excess amino acid is translocated to host tissue

N_2 gas diffuses into nodule

Figure 5.23 Root nodules of leguminous plants.

Economically important legumes

Soybean

Soybean (*Glycine max*) is a native of south-east Asia, and has an ancient history of human cultivation as a food plant in China and other countries there. Soybean did not reach the West until the seventeenth century, but now is a major world crop (Table 5.2). It grows best in warm temperate climates, and is a summer annual. Soybeans may be processed for oil used in food manufacture and other industries, and the remainder, a protein-rich cake, is used as animal feed. In human nutrition most soybean is converted into a flour and used in manufactured foods.

Table 5.2 Major crops of the world

Crop	Area harvested (million hectares)
Wheat	215
Rice	155
Maize	139
Soya*	72
Sorghum	43
Millet	36
Sugar cane	19
Potato	18
Oats	13

*A legume is fourth in the list after the three major grain crops.

Source: www.fao.org

Figure 5.24 Soybean as a crop plant.

Peanut

Peanut (*Arachis hypogaea*; Figure 5.25) is a native plant of South America that has been cultivated and mostly used elsewhere in the world (as is the case with the rubber tree, the potato and the pineapple). The peanut is also known as groundnut – this is because the fruit, which originates in the fertilised flower above ground and takes the form of a seed pod, is then pushed below the soil level by growth of the flower stalk.

Figure 5.25 Peanut crop under cultivation, and the seed pods when unearthed at harvest.

Today, most peanuts are grown in China and the USA. Peanuts contain about 50% oil and 25–30% protein. They are used for oil extraction and animal feed, as well as their uses in human consumption.

Pulses – peas and beans

The pulses are essentials in the diet of people all over the world, particularly in the Far East and Latin America, but also in North America, Europe and, to a lesser extent, Africa. The genus *Phaseolus* is the most important source of beans (scarlet runner beans, white beans, black beans and kidney beans), along with *Vicia faba* (broad bean), *Lens esculenta* (lentil), and *Pisum sativum* (green pea) (Figure 5.26).

Legumes of forage crops and pastures

The presence of legumes in forage crops (grasses) for livestock greatly increases the proportion of protein present. In terms of combating world hunger, it is infinitely preferable to enrich forage in this way, rather than feeding protein-rich grain to livestock when the latter can be used in human nutrition. In the USA, the popular legume grown as forage is alfalfa (lucerne); in the UK clover (Figure 5.27) is common.

Figure 5.26 Peas grown for animal feed uses.

Figure 5.27 Clover (*Trifolium* sp.) growing with grass.

Intensive cultivation in horticulture

Glasshouse crops

Glasshouses or greenhouses, light structures with sides and roof of glass (or transparent plastic), are used for growing delicate plants or advancing growth of certain valuable crops when the external conditions would hinder or prevent their growth. The 'glasshouse effect' (the trapping of the sun's energy by internal reflection) raises the temperature inside above the surroundings. Additionally, the air or soil in the glasshouse may be heated, and the temperature regulated. The other internal conditions – light, humidity and moisture, mineral nutrients, and even the level of carbon dioxide in the atmosphere – may also be controlled to maximise growth (or bring about flowering in ornamental plants). The major crops grown in commercial nurseries include tomatoes, peppers, cucumbers, strawberries, aubergines, courgettes and lettuces. The expense involved in this form of cultivation is justified by the higher prices paid for crops produced early or out of season.

Figure 5.28 Lettuces grown out of season in a regulated environment.

Hydroponics

Hydroponics is the growing of plants without soil (Figure 5.29), and is an extension of the glasshouse principle. Typically, plants are held in inert rooting medium, and a nutrient solution is fed to the roots as the plants grow in a carefully controlled environment. Ideally, the spent nutrient solution is recovered, analysed, replenished and then recycled. However, with the crop plants growing close together, pests including various insects, viruses and fungi may threaten, and need to be controlled. This is a highly technical and capital-intensive type of horticulture, but it may be productive. Water and land are conserved, and environmental damage due to the pollution of groundwater by nutrient run-off is prevented. In extremely arid desert locations, with excess solar radiation but limited water supplies, hydroponics is a practical way of cultivating fresh vegetables. (Here, solar radiation facilitates distillation of the required pure water from brackish water or seawater.)

There have been successes with this form of cultivation, but hydroponics may not be profitable when the costs of fuel and materials rise and/or financial returns on crops fall, in changing market conditions.

Figure 5.29 Cucumber cultivation by hydroponics, in a glasshouse.

the plants are rooted in pumice chips and supplied with nutrients in solution via a fine plastic pipe

run-off from pots is collected and recycled after nutrient composition has been adjusted

Salination of agricultural land

For the effective production of crops where there is inadequate rainfall, irrigation is required (Figure 5.31). To do this, water is carried to crops, or channelled to flow around the fields, or is pumped up and sprayed over the crops. The water in rivers was originally rainwater that has seeped through soils and flowed into contributory streams. In the process, soluble salts dissolve in the water, which is then much less pure than the original rainwater. Back in a crop field, irrigation water mostly evaporates (much is transpired by the crop plants), but the salts delivered in the irrigation stream remain behind (Figure 5.30). So irrigation is inadvertently a process that slowly brings about salination of productive soils. Unless heavy rainfall leaches out the salts and washes them to the sea, increasing salination kills the crops. Desertification of land that once was productive follows.

8 How may rising salt levels in irrigated soils lead to desertification?

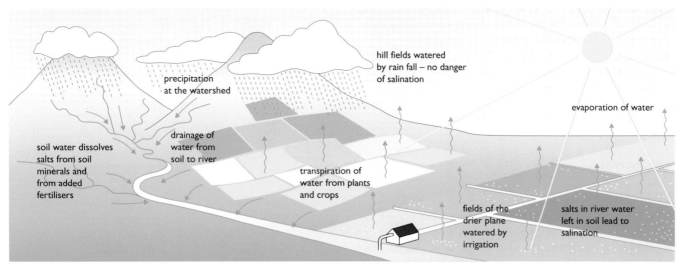

Figure 5.30 How salination occurs.

Figure 5.31 Irrigation processes in developed countries (left) and in less-developed countries (right).

The search for crop plants that can survive and thrive

Not all plants are defeated by high salt concentrations. Species we call halophytes can survive and grow in high salt concentrations (Figure 7.2, page 77). Typically, halophytes lower the water potential of their cells below that of the saline solution in which they grow. Salts are accumulated in the cell vacuole (surrounded by a special membrane, the tonoplast), away from the cytoplasm and salt-sensitive enzymes. The water potential of the cytoplasm is lowered by soluble organic ions that do not harm the cell's metabolic machinery. Salt-toleration mechanisms are genetically controlled.

The possible approaches of plant breeders to overcome this problem involve:

- screening existing varieties of crop plants for salt tolerance and breeding new varieties from the most tolerant of existing plants – the progeny are tested for evidence of increased tolerance (this is the traditional way that breeders have brought about genetic modification and the development of new, more useful varieties)
- searching for the genes for tolerance, isolation of these genes, and their transfer by means of recombinant DNA technology to produce new varieties directly – in this way existing successful varieties may be adapted to salinated soils.

Nevertheless, the problem is a serious one, of increasing importance, and with no quick solutions.

The responding plant

Sensitivity is the detection of and response to internal and environmental changes, and is a characteristic of all living things. The responses to stimuli by plants are mostly slow, growth movements (Figure 6.1); in contrast, animal responses typically involve locomotion. Nevertheless, plants are extremely sensitive – a fact that can be demonstrated at every stage of their life cycle. Plant growth, development and response are regulated by chemical messengers. It was during investigations of the effects of light on stem growth that plant hormones were first discovered. These are called plant growth **regulators**, as they are different from the hormones of animals (Table 6.1).

1 What is the difference between growth and development?

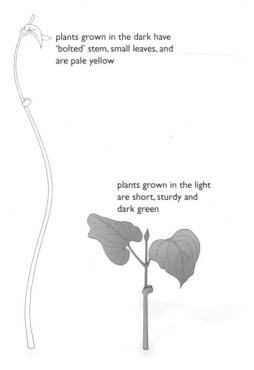

plants grown in the dark have 'bolted' stem, small leaves, and are pale yellow

plants grown in the light are short, sturdy and dark green

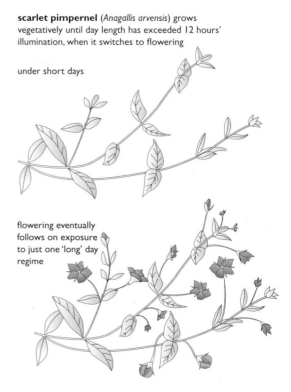

scarlet pimpernel (*Anagallis arvensis*) grows vegetatively until day length has exceeded 12 hours' illumination, when it switches to flowering

under short days

flowering eventually follows on exposure to just one 'long' day regime

Table 6.1 Differences between animal hormones and plant growth regulators

Animal hormones	Plant growth regulators
Produced in specialised cells in specific glands, e.g. insulin in Islets of Langerhans in the pancreas	Produced in unspecialised cells, in regions such as root and stem tips, leaves or buds
Transported to all parts of the body in the blood stream	Not necessarily transported widely or at all; some are active at the site of production
Effects highly specific to a particular tissue or organ (target organ/tissue) and without effect on other tissues or different organs	Not usually specific in effects, tend to influence different tissues or organs, sometimes in contrasting ways

Figure 6.1 Examples of plant sensitivity and responses.

The plant growth regulators

Indoleacetic acid (IAA), or auxin

- *Discovery* – initially by Charles Darwin, working with grass coleoptiles and their curvature towards a unilateral light source. Later, Frits Went (a Dutchman) devised a biological assay to find the concentrations in plant organs of auxin – as IAA is also known.
- *Roles* – extension growth of stems and roots (at different concentrations), dominance of terminal buds, promotion of fruit growth, and inhibition of leaf fall.
- *Synthesis* – at stem and root tips and in young leaves, from the amino acid tryptophan.

Gibberellins (GA)

- *Discovery* – initially in rice plants infected with a fungus (*Gibberella* sp.) that causes plants to bolt
- *Roles* – promotes extension growth of stems (elongation between internodes), and growth. Delays senescence of leaves/leaf fall. Inhibits lateral root initiation.
- *Synthesis* – in chloroplasts, embryos of seeds and young leaves (except in genetically dwarf varieties).

Figure 6.2 The plant growth regulators (continued overleaf).

indole acetic acid (known as 'auxin')

gibberellins e.g. gibberellic acid

Cytokinin

- *Discovery* – during investigation of growth and development of plant embryos.
- *Roles* – stimulates differentiation of cells and promotes bud formation. Delays senescence of leaves/leaf fall.
- *Synthesis* – in dividing cells of stem and root tips, from adenine (nucleic acid base).

Abscisic acid (ABA)

- *Discovery* – during investigation of bud and seed dormancy, and abscission of fruits.
- *Roles* – induction of bud and seed dormancy, and as a stress hormone, e.g. triggering stomatal closure when cells are short of water.
- *Synthesis* – in most organs of mature plants, in tiny amounts.

Ethene

- *Discovery* – as an active component in ripening fruit (subsequently confirmed using gas–liquid chromatography).
- *Roles* – promotes senescence of leaves/leaf fall (abscission), ripening of fruits and bud dormancy.
- *Synthesis* – in most organs of mature plants, in tiny amounts.

Figure 6.2 (continued) The plant growth regulators.

Interaction of plant growth regulators

Some plant growth regulators produce specific effects in tissues entirely on their own, but in many situations they interact with another growth regulator to bring about effects. Interaction may enhance an effect (**synergism**), or it may inhibit the effect (**antagonism**) (Figure 6.3).

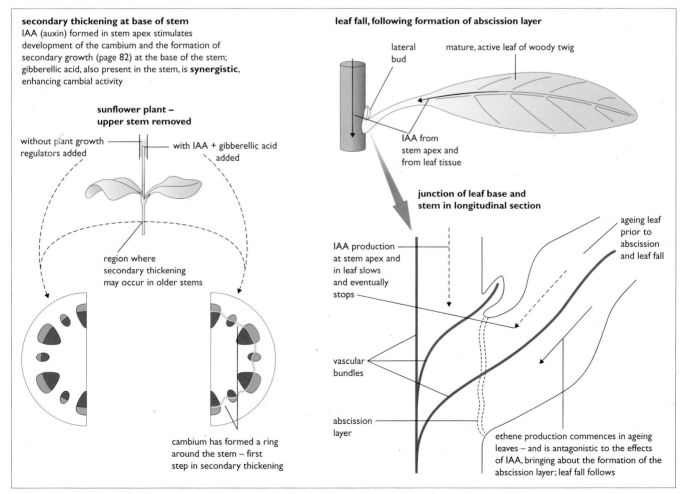

Figure 6.3 Interaction of plant growth regulators.

Dormancy

Away from the equator, plants experience **seasonal variations** in climate, particularly in light intensity, day length and temperature. Climate variations are most pronounced in **temperate zones**, where annual alternation of favourable (e.g. summer) and unfavourable (e.g. winter) seasons occurs. Here, plants typically show strategies for survival of the unfavourable season (Figure 6.4), including a dormant phase in the life cycle. Dormancy is a resting condition – a period of reduced metabolic activity due to environmental conditions (imposed) or arising from internal factors (innate).

2 As well as survival in winter conditions, a rhizome may also bring about asexual reproduction. Explain how.

life cycles

ephemerals – plants that germinate and flower quickly, whenever conditions are favourable e.g. weeds, desert plants

annuals – plants that grow from seed to seed production in one year and overwinter as seeds e.g. chickweed, shepherd's purse

biennials – plants that complete their life cycle in two years, growing from seed in the first, overwintering as a below-ground storage organ (e.g. root) with rosette of leaves and bud, and producing seed in the second year, e.g. carrot

perennials – plants that survive many years
- **woody** perennials survive the winter with a woody aerial system, protected by bark
- **herbaceous** perennials survive the winter as a below-ground stem (a rhizome) or bud (a bulb), e.g. iris, onion

Figure 6.4 Plant life cycles, and strategies for survival of the unfavourable season.

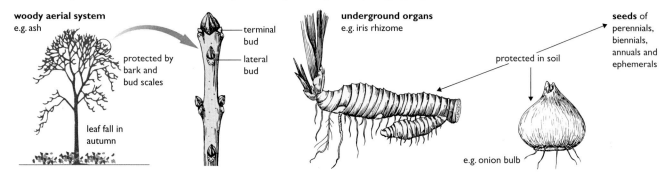

woody aerial system
e.g. ash

terminal bud

lateral bud

protected by bark and bud scales

leaf fall in autumn

underground organs
e.g. iris rhizome

protected in soil

seeds of perennials, biennials, annuals and ephemerals

e.g. onion bulb

Seed dormancy

The state of dormancy of seeds on formation typically persists beyond the dispersal stage, and may be due to a number of mechanisms (Figure 6.5).

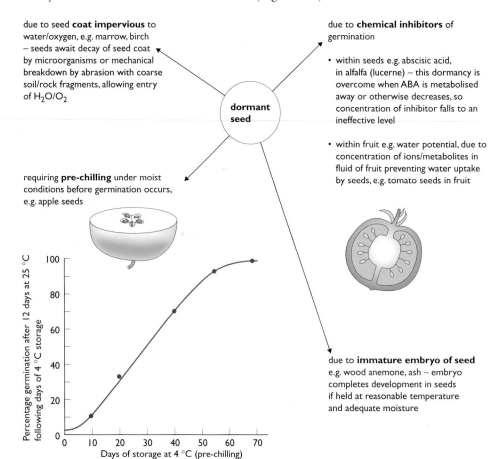

due to seed **coat impervious** to water/oxygen, e.g. marrow, birch – seeds await decay of seed coat by microorganisms or mechanical breakdown by abrasion with coarse soil/rock fragments, allowing entry of H_2O/O_2

requiring **pre-chilling** under moist conditions before germination occurs, e.g. apple seeds

dormant seed

due to **chemical inhibitors** of germination

- within seeds e.g. abscisic acid, in alfalfa (lucerne) – this dormancy is overcome when ABA is metabolised away or otherwise decreases, so concentration of inhibitor falls to an ineffective level

- within fruit e.g. water potential, due to concentration of ions/metabolites in fluid of fruit preventing water uptake by seeds, e.g. tomato seeds in fruit

due to **immature embryo of seed** e.g. wood anemone, ash – embryo completes development in seeds if held at reasonable temperature and adequate moisture

Figure 6.5 Mechanisms of seed dormancy.

Table 6.2 Conditions for germination

External	Internal
Water uptake – hydration of cytoplasm	Overcoming of dormancy mechanism (Figure 6.5)
Temperature – within optimum range for enzyme action	Production of plant growth regulators that trigger the first steps to growth and development
Oxygen – to sustain aerobic respiration	Production of hydrolytic enzymes for mobilisation of stored food reserves
Light – some seeds require exposure to light to overcome dormancy	

Seed germination and growth

The conditions necessary for germination of a dormant seed are listed in Table 6.2. The process is initiated by falling levels of abscisic acid (ABA)(growth inhibitor) as dormancy ends, and by changing levels of cytokinin and gibberellin (GA)(Figure 6.6). Germination leads to the formation of the young plant (Figures 6.7 and 6.8). IAA is inactive in breaking dormancy, but is produced at the growing points of the stem (plumule) and root (radicle), and is active in promoting their growth in length, and protein synthesis in the cells. Gibberellin is also active in germination, promoting the mobilisation of food reserves (Figure 6.7), and by stimulating leaf formation later.

3 Where is the bulk of the protein stored in the barley grain (Figure 6.7)?

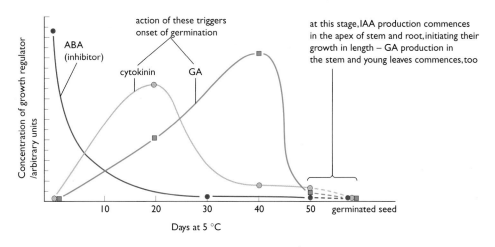

Figure 6.6 Initiation of germination in *Acer* seeds. These seeds require pre-chill treatment (5 °C) to induce germination – in response, the concentration of growth regulators in the seeds changes, leading to germination in 50 days.

Figure 6.7 Mobilisation of resources at germination.

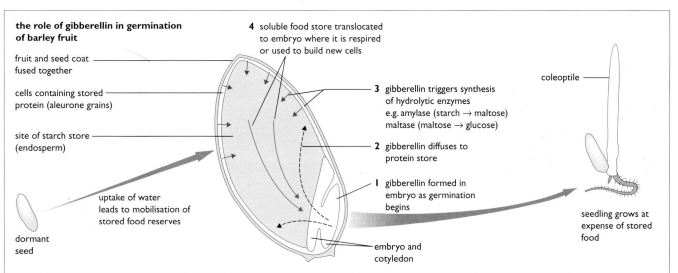

Figure 6.8 Germination of epigeal and hypogeal dicotyledonous seeds.

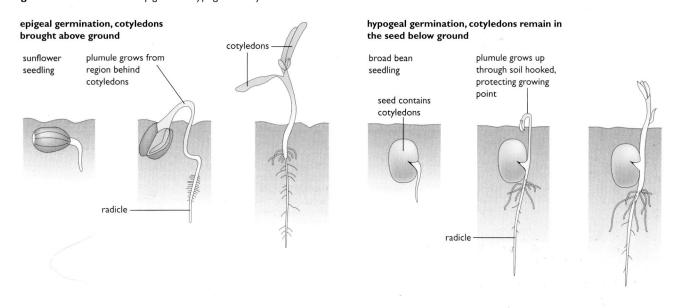

Stem and root growth – the role of IAA

Stems and roots (Figure 6.9) grow in length by cell division at the apex (stem and root tip **meristems**), followed by enlargement and development of the cells cut off behind the meristems (Figure 2.10, page 8; Figure 2.16, page 12). Cell division at the apex is promoted by indoleacetic acid (IAA) and cytokinins, operating synergistically. A high cytokinin-to-IAA ratio causes the cells to develop into bud, stem and leaf tissues; a low IAA-to-cytokinin ratio favours root formation.

Enlargement of the developing cells (extension growth) occurs further behind the apex. In stems, extension growth is triggered by IAA and GA, operating synergistically.

4 The cell cycle of a meristematic cell consists of cell growth, mitosis and division. When in the cycle are the chromosomes copied (replicated)?

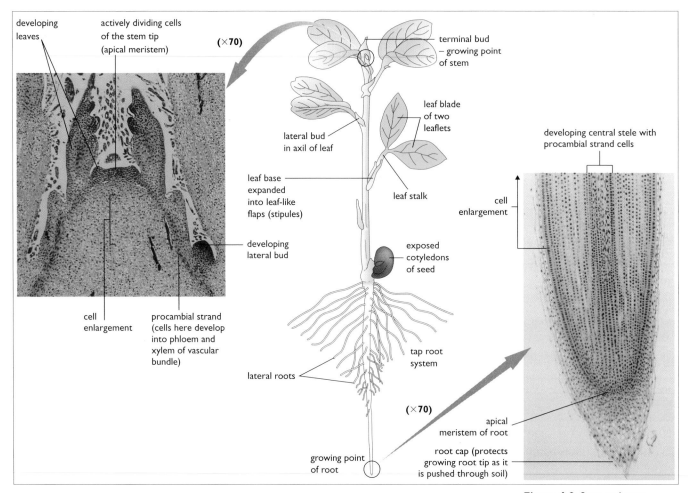

Figure 6.9 Stem and root growth in the broad bean seedling.

IAA distribution in the intact plant

Bioassays of the IAA concentration of seedlings (Figure 6.14, page 71) show that synthesis occurs at the apexes, and that the concentration falls progressively behind the tips. The stem apex produces a higher concentration than the root. It seems that IAA is used up or destroyed in growth, and is continuously replaced from the apexes – and (in the stem) from maturing leaves, too (Figure 6.10).

Figure 6.10 Distribution of IAA in the oat seedling.

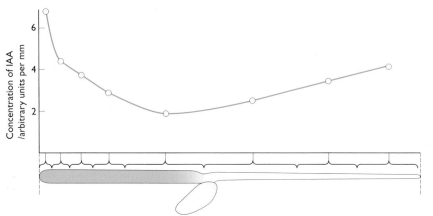

Regions of coleoptile and radicle analysed at mm intervals

Formation of lateral stems and roots

Lateral stems originate from lateral buds that 'break' and grow. The lateral buds immediately below a terminal bud that is actively growing typically remain dormant (apical dominance). Experiments in which the terminal bud is removed show us that apical dominance is due to suppression of lateral bud growth by IAA formed at the stem tip (Figure 6.11). Further down a growing stem, where the IAA concentration is lower, lateral stem formation is the norm.

Figure 6.11 Investigation of apical dominance and lateral stem formation.

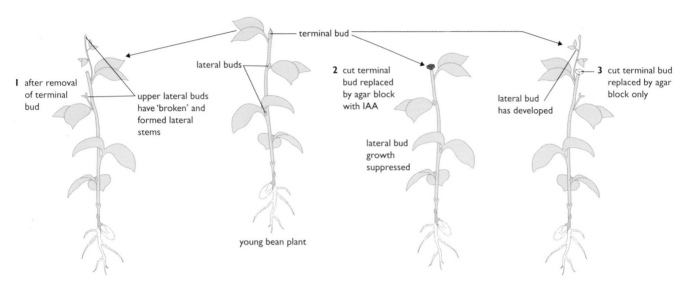

In contrast with lateral stems, **lateral roots** arise at a considerable distance behind the apex (where the concentration of IAA has fallen to a low level). Furthermore, the lateral root meristem arises in the interior of the root, in a layer of cells (pericycle) found just within the central stele. The developing lateral root pushes between the cells of the root cortex and erupts through the root epidermis (Figure 6.12).

Figure 6.12 Lateral root formation.

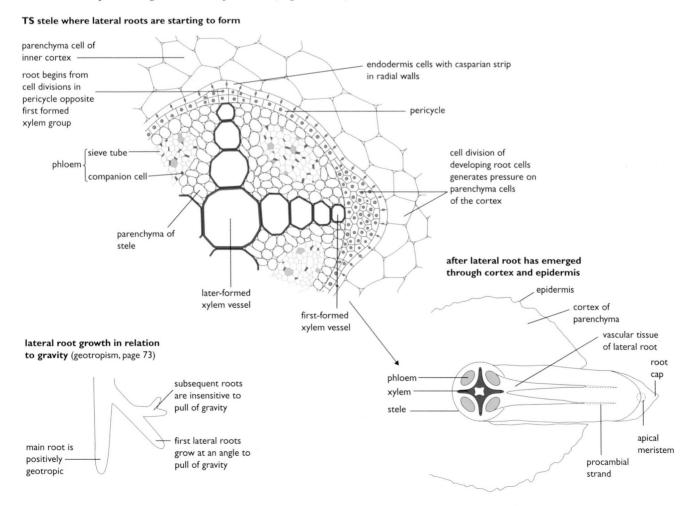

Extension: how the role of IAA in extension growth of stems was discovered

The coleoptile is a sheath of stem-like tissue found in grasses, which protects the shoot of the germinating grass as it grows up through the soil (Figure 5.20, page 58). Coleoptiles grow and respond much as stems do, but differ from stems in not bearing developing leaves, so they are easier to handle in investigations. Experiments with batches of oat coleoptiles that had been exposed to unilateral light led eventually to the discovery of auxin (Figure 6.13). Much later, auxin was isolated, analysed and identified as IAA.

Figure 6.13 Steps in the discovery of auxin.

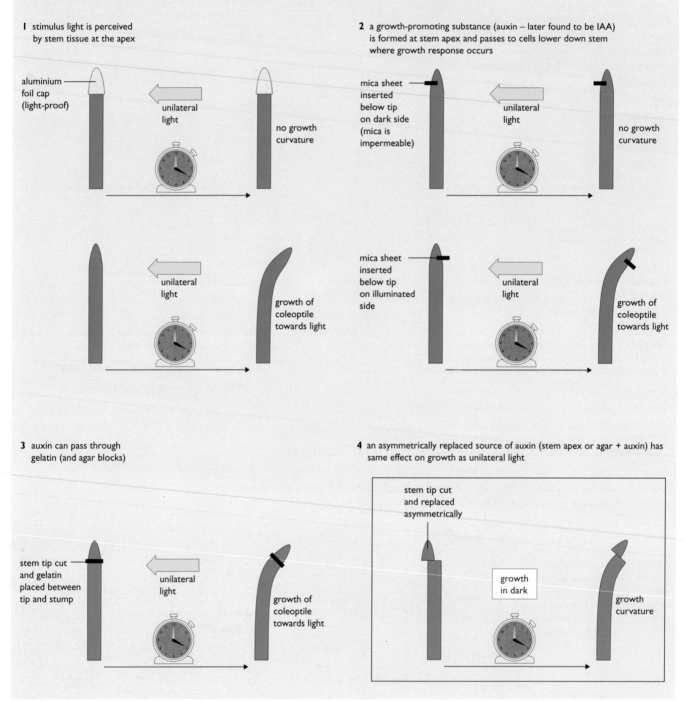

1 stimulus light is perceived by stem tissue at the apex

2 a growth-promoting substance (auxin – later found to be IAA) is formed at stem apex and passes to cells lower down stem where growth response occurs

3 auxin can pass through gelatin (and agar blocks)

4 an asymmetrically replaced source of auxin (stem apex or agar + auxin) has same effect on growth as unilateral light

Bioassay of IAA

When a freshly cut coleoptile tip is placed on an agar block, IAA diffuses out and accumulates in the agar. A Dutchman, Frits Went, exploited this discovery. He showed that when this agar block was placed on one side of a fresh coleoptile stump, the result was a growth curvature in the coleoptile. As a control, he showed that an untreated block produced no curvature. Furthermore, the degree of curvature of the coleoptile was proportional to the amount of IAA present in the agar block. Went adapted this discovery as the basis of his **bioassay of IAA concentration** (Figure 6.14).

5 Why is a bioassay necessary to estimate the concentrations of IAA found in plant tissues?

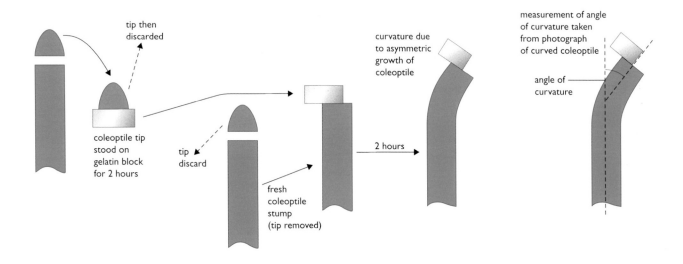

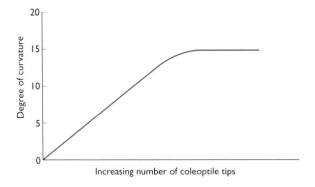

degree of curvature found to be proportional to
number of coleoptile tips stood on the gelatin block

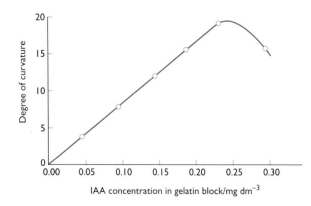

after auxin was found to be IAA, the curvature tests were
repeated with IAA in gelatin, at a range of concentrations

Figure 6.14 The oat coleoptile curvature test – a bioassay.

Commercial applications of plant growth regulators

There are numerous commercial applications of plant growth regulators. For example,
various synthetic alternatives to IAA are used as herbicides and in hormone rooting
powders. Ethene is used to ripen fruits such as apples and bananas (Figure 6.15).

2,4-D

(2,4-dichlorophenoxyacetic acid) is a
synthetic analogue of IAA used in
herbicide preparations to kill broadleaved (dicotyledonous) weeds –
increasing productivity of cultivated
grass crops (e.g. cereals) and helping
gardeners to rid lawns of weeds

NAA

(α-naphthaleneacetic acid) is a
synthetic analogue of IAA used as
'rooting hormone' – application to
cut end of stem stimulates formation
of a rooting system when treated
cuttings are planted in moist soil;
widely used in horticulture and plant
breeding research

ethene

applied to fruit that has been harvested and transported in the
unripened state (without loss of quality), causing it to ripen for
sale when market demand occurs – bananas (above) and apples
are treated in this way

Figure 6.15 Commercial applications of growth regulators.

Tropisms

A **tropism** is growth movement of a plant organ in response to an external stimulus in which the direction of the stimulus determines the direction of the response, e.g. the stem's response to unilateral light, or the response of stems and roots to gravity.

Phototropism of the aerial parts of plants

A stem tip grows towards a light – a case of positive **phototropism**. The 'solar tracking' response of leaves is also phototropism (Figure 6.16), but here the plant organs orientate at right angles to the light source.

6 Solar tracking has been described as 'the real role of phototropism'. What does this mean?

Figure 6.16 Solar tracking of the aerial parts of sunflower plants.

Investigating positive phototropism of stems

In stems and coleoptiles exposed to unilateral light, the IAA passing down the stem is redistributed and accumulates on the darkened side, causing curvature of the stem (Figure 6.17).

Figure 6.17 The role of IAA in positive phototropism.

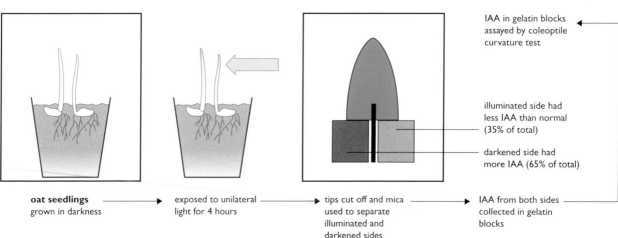

IAA in gelatin blocks assayed by coleoptile curvature test

illuminated side had less IAA than normal (35% of total)

darkened side had more IAA (65% of total)

oat seedlings grown in darkness → exposed to unilateral light for 4 hours → tips cut off and mica used to separate illuminated and darkened sides → IAA from both sides collected in gelatin blocks

explanation of positive phototropic response of stems

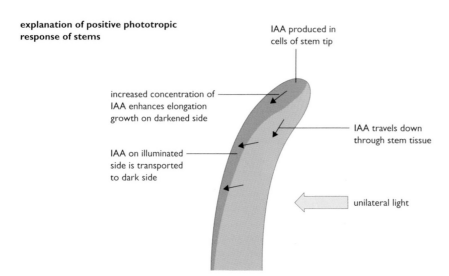

IAA produced in cells of stem tip

increased concentration of IAA enhances elongation growth on darkened side

IAA travels down through stem tissue

IAA on illuminated side is transported to dark side

unilateral light

The response to gravity – geotropism

In a seedling placed horizontally, the stem tips grow up and the main root tip grows down. This **geotropic** response is of value to any seedling accidentally planted at an angle – its growth is rapidly adjusted. But how is this response to the unilateral pull of gravity regulated – and how is it that stem and root tip respond by growth in opposite directions? An explanation involves IAA and its redistribution (Figure 6.18) – but growth inhibitors may also be involved.

Figure 6.18 The role of IAA in the geotropic response of stem and root tips.

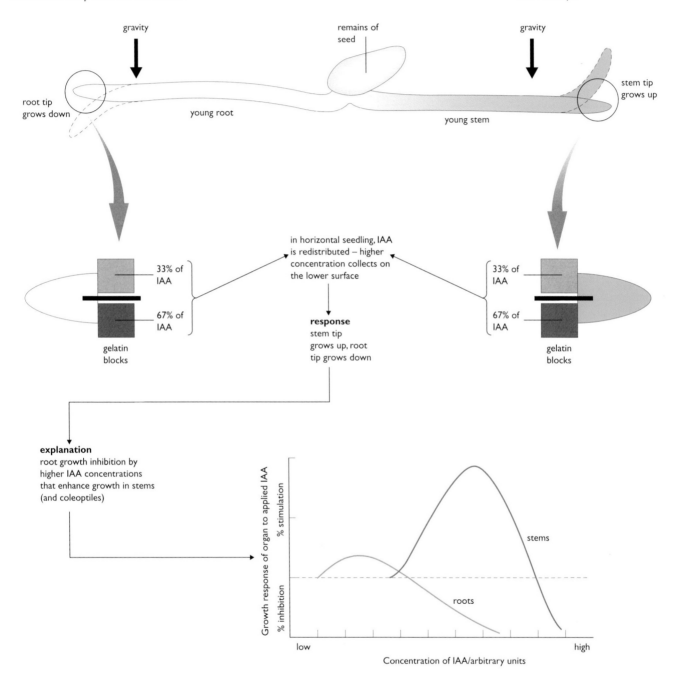

Growth inhibitors in tropic responses?

There is evidence to support another explanation of the positive geotropic response of roots. In the root apex of horizontally placed seedlings, growth inhibitor substances including abscisic acid (ABA) are produced and redistributed to the lower side of the root. Here they cause slower growth. Normal growth continues on the upper side, and the root tip as a whole grows down.

Similarly, the positive phototropic response of stems (rather than of coleoptiles) may involve growth inhibitors. On the illuminated side of a sunflower stem (*Helianthus* sp.), inactive precursors are converted to growth inhibitors that slow growth there, at least contributing to growth curvature.

Flowering

Many plants have a precise season when flowers are produced, and here it is day length that provides the important signals. This response is known as **photoperiodism**. In temperate parts of the world, such as the UK, daylight in winter may last only 8 hours, whereas it is light for 17 hours in midsummer. Plants can detect changes in day length – to within a few minutes in some cases. It is long summer days that trigger flowering in long-day plants, but short days trigger flowering in short-day plants.

Figure 6.19 Photoperiodism.

Phytochrome pigment and light

A blue-green pigment called **phytochrome** is present in green plants in low concentrations. It is a large conjugated protein, and is highly reactive. Phytochrome exists in two interconvertible forms:

- P_R – a blue pigment that absorbs mainly red light of wavelength 660 nm ($_R$ stands for red)
- P_{FR} – a blue-green pigment that absorbs mainly far-red light of wavelength 730 nm ($_{FR}$ stands for far-red).

When P_R is exposed to light (or red light on its own), it is converted to P_{FR}. In the dark (or if exposed to far-red light alone), it is converted back to P_R.

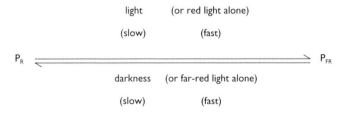

Phytochrome is the pigment system involved in photoperiodism, and P_{FR} is the active form in triggering the onset of flowering. We know this because the red/far-red absorption spectrum of phytochrome corresponds to the action spectrum of light that switches off flowering in short-day plants, and switches on flowering in long-day plants.

7 Phytochrome is a conjugated protein. What are conjugated proteins, and what others do you know of?

Flowering and phytochrome

Short-day plants – flower only if the period of darkness is longer than a certain critical length. If darkness is interrupted by a brief flash of red light the plant will not flower, but this is reversed by a flash of far-red light.

Interpretation – phytochrome in P_{FR} form inhibits flowering in short-day plants. The very long nights required by short-day plants allow the concentration of P_{FR} to fall to a low level, removing inhibition. A flash of light in the darkness reverses this, but then a flash of far-red light reverses it again, and flowering still takes place.

Long-day plants – flower only if the period of uninterrupted darkness is less than a certain critical length each day.

Interpretation – phytochrome in P_{FR} form promotes flowering in long-day plants. The long period of daylight causes the accumulation of P_{FR}, because P_R is converted to P_{FR}.

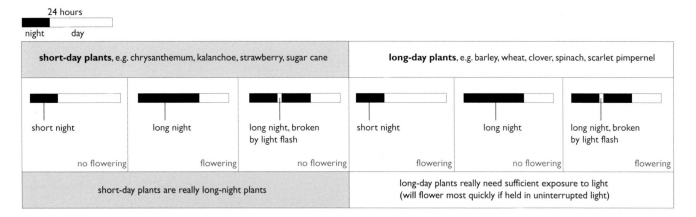

Figure 6.20 Flowering related to day-length.

Conversion of vegetative buds to flower buds

It is the leaves of plants that are sensitive to day length, yet the structural switch to flowering occurs in the stem apex (in buds). A growth regulator substance is formed in leaves under the correct regime of light and dark, and is then transported to the stem apex where it causes the switch in development. The evidence for this is that a leaf that has been exposed to the correct photoperiod, grafted onto another (non-induced) plant of the same type, will cause flowering there. So a hormone is believed to exist, and has been named **'florigen'**, but has not been isolated. As it is P_{FR} that influences a switch to flowering, this substance might work by causing the formation of a hormone that promotes the formation of florigen in long-day plants but inhibits its formation in short-day plants. However, much remains to be discovered about the control of flowering.

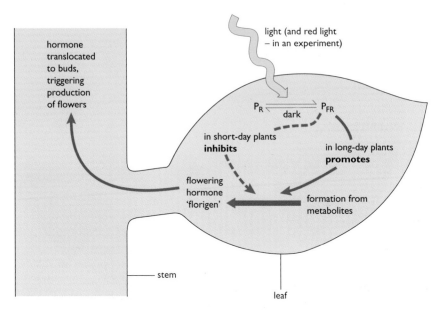

Figure 6.21 Phytochrome and flowering – a suggested hypothesis.

8 We can now see that light has diverse effects on plants. Make a concise table summarising the main effects that light has on flowering plant metabolism, and on their growth and development.

The adapted plant

Water supply

In temperate and tropical zones (such as the UK), most native plants and most crop plants are **mesophytes**, adapted to an adequate water supply. They grow best in well-drained soils with their aerial systems exposed to moderately dry air. The structure of the mesophytic leaf is shown in Figures 2.3 and 2.4 (pages 4–5). On the other hand, some plants are adapted to conditions of inadequate or erratic water supply.

Drought resistance – xerophytes

Plants adapted to survive drought are called **xerophytes**, and their special features are called **xeromorphic features** (Table 7.1). Sorghum is a grain plant of arid habitats with xeromorphic features (Figure 5.16, page 56). Marram grass is a xerophyte of sand dunes (Figure 7.1).

Table 7.1 Xeromorphic features – a summary (most xerophytes typically have some, but not all, of these features)

Xeromorphic feature	Effect
Thick cuticle to leaf and stem epidermal cells	Prevents water loss through walls
Layer of hairs on epidermis	Traps moist air over leaf and reduces diffusion
Leaves in a rosette at ground level	Leaves held close together in moist air
Reduction in number of stomata	Reduces outlets through which moist air can diffuse
Stomata in pits or grooves	Moist air trapped outside stomata, reducing diffusion
Leaves reduced to scales/leaf rolled or folded when short of water	Reduced area from which transpiration can occur
Ability to obtain water when scarce, using: • superficial roots • deep and extensive roots	Exploits overnight condensation Exploits deep water table in soil

Figure 7.1 Marram grass (*Ammophila arenaria*).

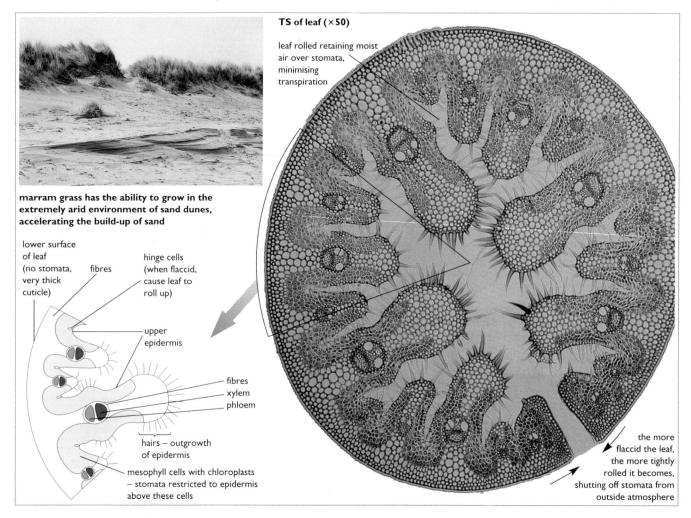

marram grass has the ability to grow in the extremely arid environment of sand dunes, accelerating the build-up of sand

TS of leaf (×50)

leaf rolled retaining moist air over stomata, minimising transpiration

lower surface of leaf (no stomata, very thick cuticle)

fibres

hinge cells (when flaccid, cause leaf to roll up)

upper epidermis

fibres
xylem
phloem

hairs – outgrowth of epidermis

mesophyll cells with chloroplasts – stomata restricted to epidermis above these cells

the more flaccid the leaf, the more tightly rolled it becomes, shutting off stomata from outside atmosphere

Plants of salt marshes – halophytes

Halophytes are plants adapted to the high-salt environments of salt marshes and estuaries, where they grow in soils irrigated by seawater. At times the plants may be inundated by high tides. Here, too, the degree of salinity may be extremely variable. Once the tide recedes, the salt concentration of the seawater trapped in pools and channels may be concentrated by evaporation. Alternatively, these waters may be diluted by heavy rainfall, and by an excess of river water flowing from the land (Figure 7.2). Typically, successful salt marsh plants:

- may be succulents, storing water in their tissues, e.g. glasswort (*Salicornia* spp.)
- retain a concentration of salts in their cells higher than in seawater, so that water uptake by osmosis can still occur
- show xeromorphic features in their aerial systems (stems and leaves), such as a thick, waxy cuticle, by which water loss by transpiration is reduced
- have extensive air spaces in stems and roots that are continuous and connected – these maintain aerobic conditions internally, including in roots that may grow in waterlogged soils, and make the stems and leaves buoyant when submerged by high tides.

I Halophytes may grow in waterlogged soils, yet they typically show xeromorphic features. Why are such features advantageous?

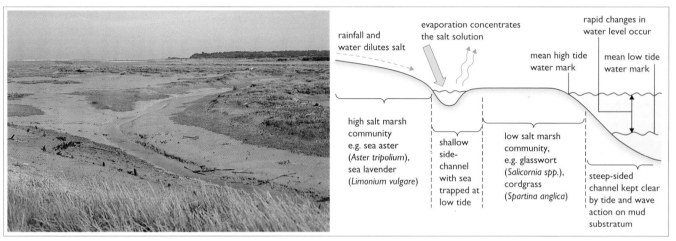

Figure 7.2 The features of the salt marsh environment.

Figure 7.3 Salt marsh plants.

Aquatic plants – hydrophytes

Water is a dense medium that provides support for the submerged or floating parts of aquatic plants. The large air spaces in the stems and leaves of these plants are gas reservoirs for respiration and photosynthesis (Figures 7.4 and 7.5). Also, they make the plant organs buoyant, so leaves float at or near the surface for better illumination. The cuticle is thin or absent, and stomata occur on the upper surface of floating leaves.

Figure 7.4 *Nymphaea alba* (water lily) – the structure of a floating leaf.

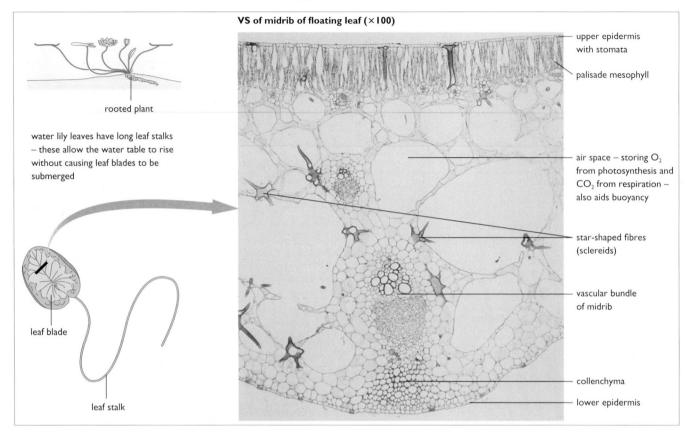

VS of midrib of floating leaf (×100)

rooted plant

water lily leaves have long leaf stalks – these allow the water table to rise without causing leaf blades to be submerged

leaf blade

leaf stalk

upper epidermis with stomata

palisade mesophyll

air space – storing O_2 from photosynthesis and CO_2 from respiration – also aids buoyancy

star-shaped fibres (sclereids)

vascular bundle of midrib

collenchyma

lower epidermis

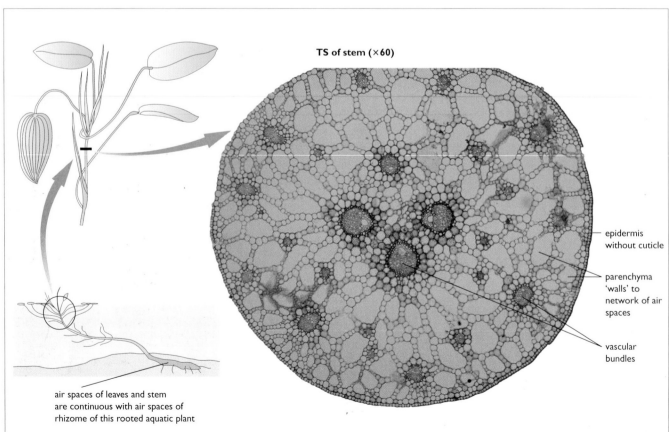

TS of stem (×60)

air spaces of leaves and stem are continuous with air spaces of rhizome of this rooted aquatic plant

epidermis without cuticle

parenchyma 'walls' to network of air spaces

vascular bundles

Figure 7.5 *Potamogeton natans* (broadleaved pondweed) – stem structure.

Mineral nutrition

The role of ions in green plant metabolism is summarised in Figure 2.2 (page 3). The usual sources of mineral ions in soils are shown in Figure 2.24 (page 17). In environments where the supply of ions is inadequate for some reason, adaptations that maintain a supply of essential mineral ions are invaluable.

Carnivorous plants

On mountains, low temperatures slow the decay of dead organisms. Ions, when they are released, tend to be washed away by the high rainfall. However, carnivorous plants (e.g. Figure 7.6) can trap minibeasts, and take essential ions from their decaying or digested bodies.

2 What are the likely fates of the soluble ions of soil, such as nitrates and potassium ions, if the root cells of flowering plants fail to absorb them?

Figure 7.6 Sundew (*Drosera*) in a Scottish peat bog.

the common sundew is frequent in bogs where *Sphagnum* also grows – its rosette of leaves traps small creatures, and stalked glandular hairs secrete a glistening liquid that entices and traps animals

as the animal struggles, hairs bend over and secrete more liquid; the animal is trapped, dies, and its organs are digested by proteases, lipases and carbohydrases secreted by the glands – the chitin exoskeleton is not digested, but eventually is blown away; amino acids, fatty acids, sugars and ions are absorbed by gland cells of the leaf that secreted the enzymes

Mycorrhiza

Some ions are released by decay at times in the year when plants have least need for them. On the other hand, when they are most required by plants, competition for ions is greatest. Perhaps in response to this, many plants live in close mutualistic relationship with a species of fungus in which the fungus absorbs and hoards ions as soon as they become available, and later releases them to root cells in exchange for sugar. This nutritional alliance is called an **ectotrophic mycorrhiza** (Figure 7.7).

Figure 7.7 The structure and functioning of an ectotrophic mycorrhiza.

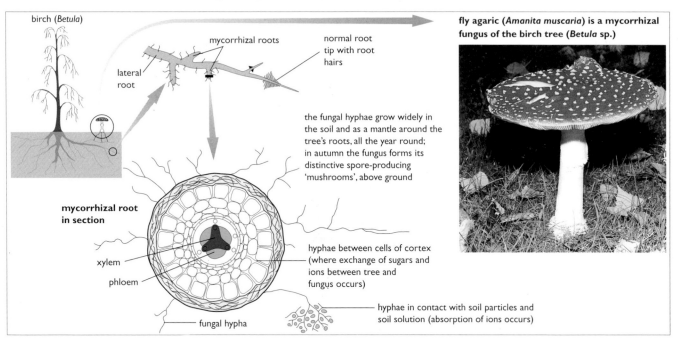

birch (*Betula*)

mycorrhizal roots

normal root tip with root hairs

lateral root

fly agaric (*Amanita muscaria*) is a mycorrhizal fungus of the birch tree (*Betula* sp.)

the fungal hyphae grow widely in the soil and as a mantle around the tree's roots, all the year round; in autumn the fungus forms its distinctive spore-producing 'mushrooms', above ground

mycorrhizal root in section

xylem

phloem

hyphae between cells of cortex (where exchange of sugars and ions between tree and fungus occurs)

fungal hypha

hyphae in contact with soil particles and soil solution (absorption of ions occurs)

Predation by browsers

Being rooted to the ground, a plant is vulnerable to the persistent attentions of predatory herbivores that may browse on the leaves, buds, stems or root tissues, causing harm to the plant. However, plants show adaptations that may be effective defences.

Physical defences – thorns and prickles

Large browsing animals need to eat quantities of leafy shoots and grind them up prior to digestion. Browsing may be discouraged by modification of lateral shoots, leaf bases or parts of leaves into sharp, pointed structures that can harm the mouth or gut of the herbivore, such as prickles at the edges of holly leaves, stem spines of gorse, or the spines of thistles (Figure 7.8).

Figure 7.8 Spear thistles (*Cirsium vulgare*).

Behavioural defences – using ants

Tropical acacia trees have a protective association with ants. The trees have leaf stalks modified as extra-floral nectaries that provide sugar solution, and glandular cells that secrete protein solution at the tips of leaflets. These are food sources taken by the ants. In turn, their permanent presence on the acacia plants wards off a range of browsers, because of the ants' vicious sting (Figure 7.9).

Figure 7.9 Tropical acacia and its army of protective ants.

Chemical defences – in stings

The stings of the common nettle each function as an injection syringe and deliver a cocktail of irritating and poisonous chemicals (Figure 7.10).

Figure 7.10 The stings of the common nettle (*Urtica dioica*).

Chemical defences – in tissues

A great variety of chemical compounds may provide protection against other organisms. Some are highly toxic and kill predators when consumed in small doses – for example, alkaloids in rhododendrons. Others are cumulative in their effects, such as tannins of oaks and many other plants, which are protein precipitants – making food less digestible and causing starvation and stunting. The plant *Pyrethrum*, a relative of the chrysanthemum, produces a terpene that is a natural insecticide (the genes for which genetic engineers seek to transfer to other crop plants). Bracken is a fern with exceptionally effective chemical protection (Figure 7.11).

bracken leaves contain:

- an inhibitor of seed germination (released into the soil and leaf litter around the plant)
- an insect moulting hormone (interferes in growth of insects browsing on the plant)
- an enzyme destroying B vitamins in animals that eat the bracken
- a carcinogen active in cattle that feed on bracken and which they secrete in milk taken for human consumption

Figure 7.11 Chemical defence mechanisms in bracken.

Defences must fail – in the long term, at least!

Herbivores must overcome defence mechanisms of green plants or themselves fail to survive, as all food webs testify (Figure 3.2, page 24). Either a defence mechanism is overcome, in part, in the lifetime of the plant, or on death its nutrients enter the food chain. But plants themselves respond to the ravages of browsing in different ways (e.g. Figure 7.12).

Figure 7.12 Holly leaf – parasitism and recovery.

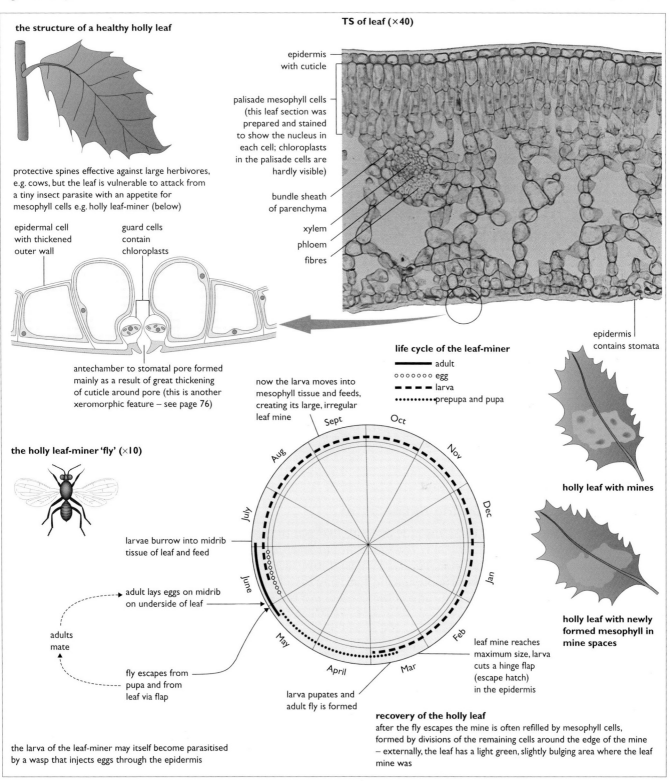

the structure of a healthy holly leaf

protective spines effective against large herbivores, e.g. cows, but the leaf is vulnerable to attack from a tiny insect parasite with an appetite for mesophyll cells e.g. holly leaf-miner (below)

epidermal cell with thickened outer wall

guard cells contain chloroplasts

antechamber to stomatal pore formed mainly as a result of great thickening of cuticle around pore (this is another xeromorphic feature – see page 76)

the holly leaf-miner 'fly' (×10)

larvae burrow into midrib tissue of leaf and feed

adult lays eggs on midrib on underside of leaf

adults mate

fly escapes from pupa and from leaf via flap

larva pupates and adult fly is formed

the larva of the leaf-miner may itself become parasitised by a wasp that injects eggs through the epidermis

TS of leaf (×40)

epidermis with cuticle

palisade mesophyll cells (this leaf section was prepared and stained to show the nucleus in each cell; chloroplasts in the palisade cells are hardly visible)

bundle sheath of parenchyma

xylem

phloem

fibres

epidermis contains stomata

life cycle of the leaf-miner
—— adult
ooooooo egg
– – – larva
•••••••• prepupa and pupa

now the larva moves into mesophyll tissue and feeds, creating its large, irregular leaf mine

Sept   Oct
Aug   Nov
July   Dec
June   Jan
May   Feb
April   Mar

leaf mine reaches maximum size, larva cuts a hinge flap (escape hatch) in the epidermis

holly leaf with mines

holly leaf with newly formed mesophyll in mine spaces

recovery of the holly leaf
after the fly escapes the mine is often refilled by mesophyll cells, formed by divisions of the remaining cells around the edge of the mine – externally, the leaf has a light green, slightly bulging area where the leaf mine was

Oak defoliation by caterpillars of the moth *Tortrix* – and the response

Oak tree leaves are predated by the browsing caterpillar of the moth *Tortrix*. In some years the attack is so heavy that oak trees are completely defoliated. The effect on oak twigs of the absence of young leaves is to trigger the 'breaking' of the buds that are forming at that stage (containing the beginnings of next year's foliage leaves). Defoliated trees form a second set of foliage leaves in summer by this mechanism.

Woody plants

Secondary thickening – what, why and where?

In large, annual dicotyledonous plants such as the sunflower, the base of the stem may undergo a process called **secondary thickening**. Secondary thickening results in additional xylem and phloem tissue being formed in rows. The additional tissues enhance the transport of water and sugar in the plant, and greatly strengthen the stem. The advantage of this can be seen in the case of a mature, flowering sunflower plant with its bulky capitulum to support (Figure 8.1).

Figure 8.1 Primary and secondary growth in the sunflower (*Helianthus annuus*).

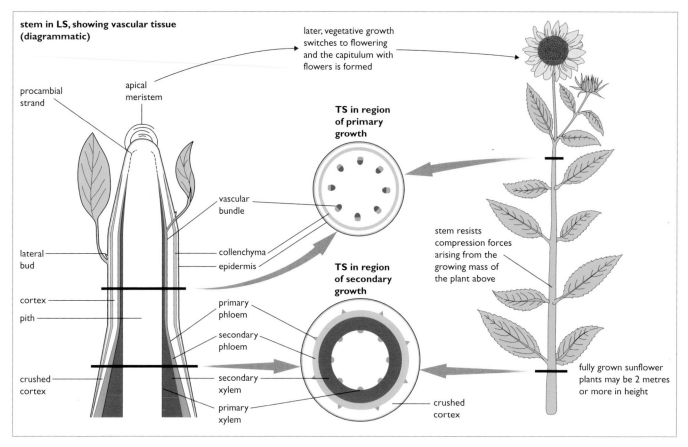

Steps to secondary thickening of the stem

First, the cambium within the vascular bundles is extended between the bundles as a result of a line of parenchyma cells becoming meristematic. The result is a complete ring of vascular cambium between cortex and pith, called a **lateral meristem** (in contrast to the apical meristems of buds) (Figure 8.2).

Figure 8.2 Formation of the ring of vascular cambium.

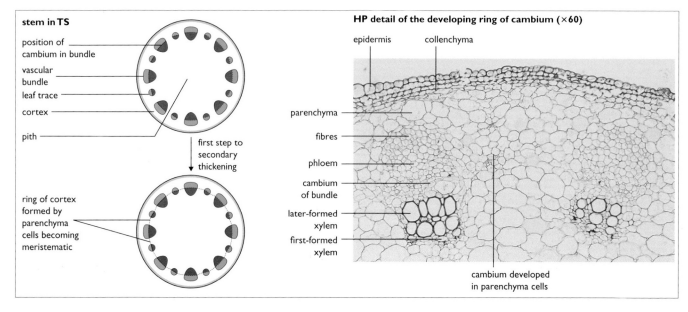

Then the cells of the ring of cambium divide repeatedly, cutting off cells to the inside and outside of the ring. The inner cells differentiate into **secondary xylem**, and the outer cells into **secondary phloem** (Figure 8.3).

Figure 8.3 Formation of secondary xylem and phloem.

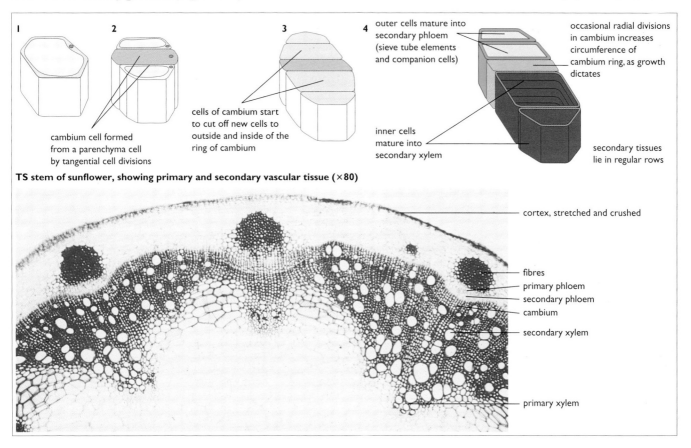

TS stem of sunflower, showing primary and secondary vascular tissue (×80)

- cortex, stretched and crushed
- fibres
- primary phloem
- secondary phloem
- cambium
- secondary xylem
- primary xylem

Secondary growth – consequences

The cambium cuts off more cells towards the inside to differentiate into xylem tissue than it does to the outside to become phloem. The presence of secondary tissues squashes the cortex, and pressure on the epidermis is very great. (In trees, a bark of cork cells forms here – page 86).

The cambium also cuts off columns of parenchyma cells, called **medullary rays** (Figure 8.4). Ray cells connect the pith with the cortex, facilitating movement of nutrients between the vascular tissues and the pith and cortex.

1 How does a cambium cell differ from a parenchyma cell?

Figure 8.4 Mature secondary tissues – the role of 'rays'.

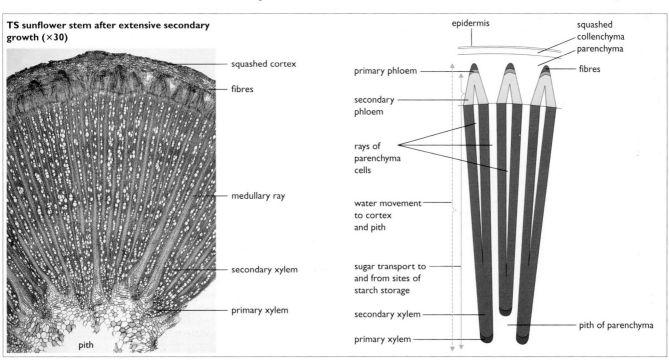

TS sunflower stem after extensive secondary growth (×30)

- squashed cortex
- fibres
- medullary ray
- secondary xylem
- primary xylem
- pith

- epidermis
- squashed collenchyma
- parenchyma
- primary phloem
- fibres
- secondary phloem
- rays of parenchyma cells
- water movement to cortex and pith
- sugar transport to and from sites of starch storage
- secondary xylem
- primary xylem
- pith of parenchyma

Woody plants – trees and shrubs

Tree and shrub species (woody plants) form a complete ring of vascular cambium in the stem as they germinate from seed, so all the vascular tissue of a tree is secondary tissue, formed in regular rows (Figure 8.5). The stem of a woody plant persists from year to year, and additional secondary xylem and phloem are formed each year. In temperate climates, growth occurs in spring and summer. The first-formed xylem each season has large, thin-walled vessels and fibres, and is called the **early wood**. Later in the growing period, the vessels and fibres are smaller and thick-walled, and are called the **late wood**. This late wood has a dense, dark appearance and gives the **annual growth ring**.

2 What are the component tissues of the bark of trees?

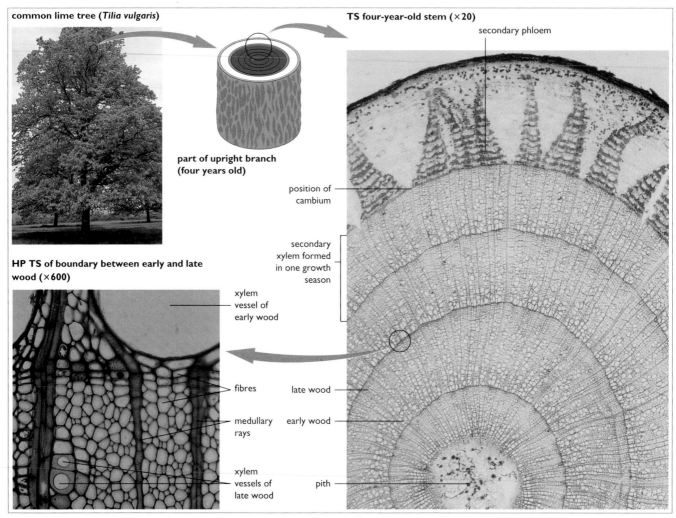

Figure 8.5 The common lime tree and the structure of the stem.

Extension: reaction wood

The wood in branches growing at an angle to the main trunk experiences compression stress below and tension stress above. The result in broadleaved (dicotyledonous) trees is known as reaction wood (Figure 8.6).

Figure 8.6 Reaction wood of lime.

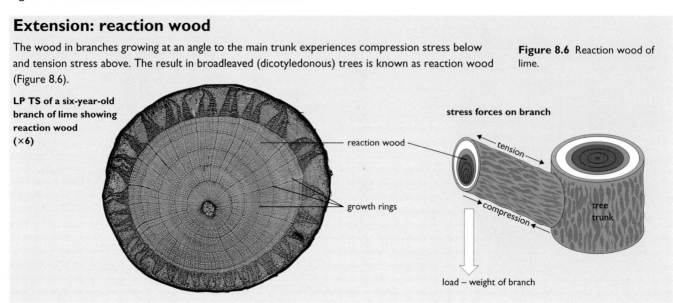

Medullary rays of wood

Columns of parenchyma cells called medullary rays (Figure 8.7) connect the living cells of cortex and pith with the functioning secondary xylem and phloem. Rays are formed by the radial division of ray initials formed in the ring of cambium.

Figure 8.7 The formation of medullary rays in ash wood (*Fraxinus excelsior*).

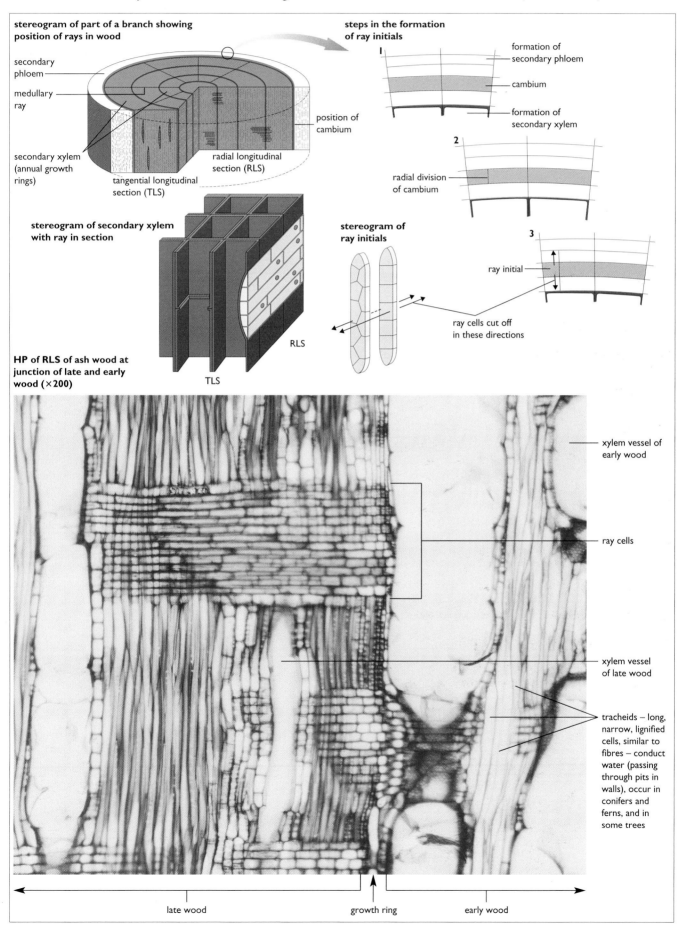

stereogram of part of a branch showing position of rays in wood

secondary phloem

medullary ray

secondary xylem (annual growth rings)

tangential longitudinal section (TLS)

radial longitudinal section (RLS)

position of cambium

steps in the formation of ray initials

1

formation of secondary phloem

cambium

formation of secondary xylem

2

radial division of cambium

stereogram of secondary xylem with ray in section

RLS

TLS

stereogram of ray initials

3

ray initial

ray cells cut off in these directions

HP of RLS of ash wood at junction of late and early wood (×200)

xylem vessel of early wood

ray cells

xylem vessel of late wood

tracheids — long, narrow, lignified cells, similar to fibres — conduct water (passing through pits in walls), occur in conifers and ferns, and in some trees

late wood

growth ring

early wood

Cork and lenticels

In trees and shrubs, the epidermis and cortex are under increasing pressure from the growth of secondary vascular tissues, and are normally replaced in the first year by cork tissue. **Cork cells** are dead, empty rectangular 'boxes' without air spaces between them, and with walls lined internally by a waxy substance, suberin. Cork is impervious to water and gases, and resistant to mechanical damage and attack by microorganisms. Cork is formed from a **cork cambium** – a second lateral cambium formed in woody plants. The cork cambium arises in the outer cortex. Cork tissue may contain **lenticels** – areas where the cork cambium has produced loosely arranged, rounded cells with air spaces between (Figures 8.8 and 8.9). Lenticels aid gas exchange, as the air spaces here are continuous with those of the cortex.

Figure 8.8 Bark of trees in semi-arid climates.

in this environment, the danger of water loss is high, so here the bark of trees is intensely smooth and waxy, with restricted, compact lenticels – the lenticels facilitate sufficient gas exchange by diffusion with minimal loss of water vapour

Figure 8.9 TS stem of lilac (*Syringa vulgaris*) showing cork and lenticels in section. Lilac is a mesophytic tree (page 76), well adapted to conditions of adequate water supply.

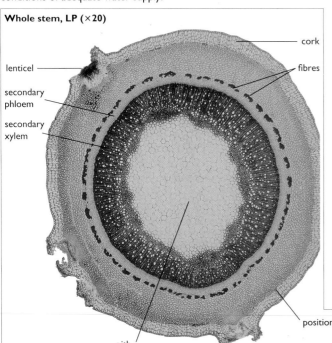

Whole stem, LP (×20)

- cork
- lenticel
- fibres
- secondary phloem
- secondary xylem
- position of cork cambium
- pith (parenchyma)

- hard smooth waxy bark
- scar of former leaf/lateral branch
- compact lenticels

TS of a lenticel, HP (×175)

- loose parenchyma cells of the lenticel
- epidermis (cut off from nutrient supply by the cork, this layer of cells dies and eventually sloughs off)
- cork cells with suberised (waxy) walls
- cork cambium

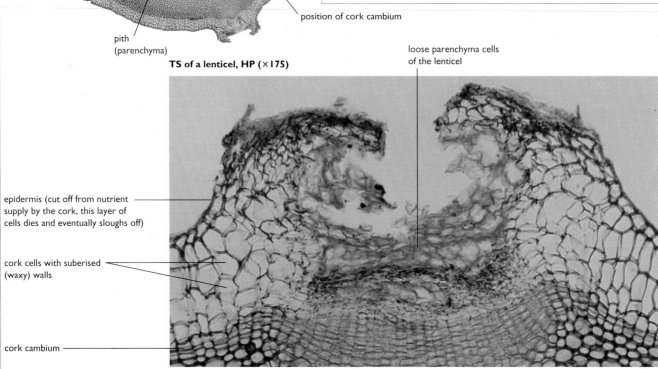

Extension: dendrochronology

Figure 8.10 The pattern of annual growth rings in an oak tree, felled in 2000.

A tree forms annual growth rings, wide in favourable years, narrower in unfavourable years (Figure 8.10). All trees of the same species in an area tend to show similar patterns of rings. Furthermore, a living tree aged, say, 250 years shares a common pattern of 150 rings with a tree of the same species, felled in the same locality 100 years ago. This is the basis of dendrochronology (the study of the age of trees by counting/measuring the annual growth rings).

The dendrochronologist, by comparing numerous examples of overlapping patterns of wood harvested in a particular area, builds up local sequences running back for thousands of years. Cross-matchings are never identical, as there are some variations from tree to tree in the same area, perhaps because of local climate differences, caterpillar action, fires, and the effects of nearby, competing trees, for example.

Oak is a long-lived tree, and cut oak wood also survives well in buildings, in archaeological sites, and in bogs and river gravels. The longest British chronology for oak extends back 7000 years, and in Germany, oak chronologies extend back 9500 years. Once such master chronologies are on record, dendrochronologists can measure the patterns of rings found in ancient samples of unknown age, matching them with the master chronology using a computer (Figure 8.11). Samples can be dated, often quite precisely, provided they are of 100 annual rings or more. Today, sophisticated computer programmes pick up underlying patterns from most local 'noise', and sometimes permit matching of patterns with samples from other parts of the country where different conditions were experienced. The science of dendrochronology has served as a check on radiocarbon dating of organic remains (the latter are accurate to within only 20 years). Dendrochronology is also a sound source of information on past climates – particularly useful for periods when no human records were kept.

Figure 8.11 Matching patterns of tree rings – the basis of dendrochronology.

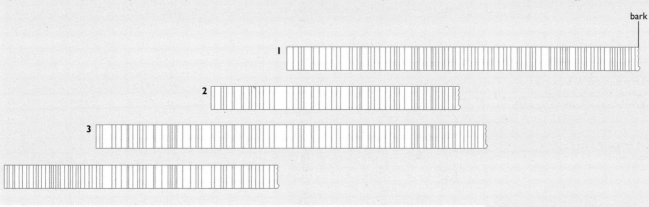

in a living tree (such as tree **1**) the year a particular ring grew can be calculated by counting back from the bark – if the pattern of wide and narrow rings can be matched to pieces of dead wood (**2–4**), they can also be dated, and in this way long chronologies can be built up

Answers

Chapter 1

1

Prokaryote cells	Eukaryote cells
Cells are small, about 5–10 μm	Cells larger, typically 50–150 μm
Nucleus absent, circular DNA helix in cytoplasm	Nucleus with nuclear membrane, with chromosomes of linear DNA
Few organelles	Many organelles
Protein synthesis in small ribosomes	Protein synthesis in large ribosomes
Some have simple flagella	Some have cilia or flagella with a 9 + 2 arrangement of microtubules

2 See 'Photosynthesis – the process' and Figures 3.1 and 3.2, page 24.

Chapter 2

1 Heterotrophs take in organic matter and digest it prior to absorption, whereas autotrophs manufacture organic matter using an energy source and simple molecules such as CO_2 and H_2O.

2 Nucleus, plus mitochondria, ribosomes, endoplasmic reticulum and Golgi apparatus.

3 Water potential (ψ) = solute potential (ψ_s) + pressure potential (ψ_p). It is the tendency of water molecules to enter or leave a solution by osmosis.

4 Cause a turgid (rigid, upright) herbaceous aerial system (stem + leaves) to wilt in warm dry air, and observe the response.

5 Toluidine blue stains lignified walls in stem/root sections greenish blue/bright blue.

6 The shape of the cellulose polymer allows close-packing into long chains held together by hydrogen bonds. These can be laid down in porous sheets, and have great tensile strength.

7 Cut thin sections from stems of the aerial system of a herbaceous plant after it has been standing in the light in a dilute solution of red ink, and examine them microscopically to find which tissue is stained red.

8 Cropping removes ions from the soil permanently. They are replaced by the application of artificial fertiliser or rotted dung or compost, at times favourable to the growing crop.

9 The forces generated in the leaves by the transpiration of water apply high tension to the water column in all xylem vessels of the trunk, causing them to shrink in diameter (but recover again overnight/when transpiration stops – see graph below).

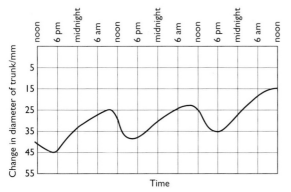

10 a) Changes as a procambial strand cell matures into a xylem vessel:
- after the cell enlarges and vacuoles appear in the cytoplasm, softening and chemical breakdown of the materials of the end (transverse) walls begins
- to the longitudinal walls, secondary cell wall materials (cellulose with lignin) are laid down
- additional wall layers in the first-formed xylem are as rings or spiral-shaped thickening, but later-formed xylem has more massive thickenings, with pits
- finally, the end walls and cell contents break down, leaving continuous tubes.

b) Changes as a procambial strand cell matures into a sieve tube element:
- after the cell enlarges and vacuoles appear in the cytoplasm, an unequal longitudinal division occurs cutting off a narrow companion cell from the sieve tube element
- secondary walls of cellulose added are thinner than the thickenings seen in the xylem, and no lignin is added
- end (transverse) walls of the sieve tube element develop pores and form a sieve plate, and cytoplasmic connections form between sieve tube elements and companion cells
- cytoplasm loses its nucleus and many of its organelles.

11 By denaturing the protein components of the cytoplasm of sieve tube elements and their companion cells, inactivating the cell's enzymes, for example.

Chapter 3

1 It is consumed in respiration to 'fuel' all the activities and functions of the carnivore.

2 The Bunsen burner used to boil water is turned off before organic solvents (e.g. propanone) are poured out. Otherwise, good laboratory practice will be sufficient to take account of any hazards and avoid significant risk.

3 The reactions in chloroplasts that release oxygen are studied directly, rather than the net output of oxygen from photosynthetic cells (where oxygen uptake in respiration also occurs, for example).

4 Because chemical reactions are highly temperature sensitive, whereas photochemical steps are relatively temperature insensitive.

5 Photosynthesis is a continuous process, but it is the sequence of reactions of CO_2 fixation that is sought. The reactants that become radioactive in turn, following uptake of brief input of labelled carbon, may disclose that sequence.

Chapter 4

1 Nectar, supplied by the buttercup flower, is a dilute solution of sucrose (and possibly of ethanol, due to the activity of yeasts), and pollen contains proteins, lipids and carbohydrates in small quantities, as does all cytoplasm.

2 A buttercup leaf (a dicotyledon) has an upper and lower surface, with the mesophyll arranged as a 'palisade' layer below the upper epidermis. The veins supplying the mesophyll are arranged as a network. Most stomata typically occur in the lower epidermis.

A ryegrass leaf (a monocotyledon) has a leaf blade that is strap-shaped, with mesophyll cells distributed evenly . The veins run parallel though the mesophyll, connected by cross branches. Stomata occur evenly distributed in the epidermis.

3 Desiccation, and exposure of the DNA of the nuclei to UV light.

4 i) By independent assortment of maternal and paternal chromosomes in meiosis I.
ii) Due to crossing over of segments of individual maternal and paternal homologous chromosomes in meiosis I.

5 Pollination is the transfer of pollen from the stamens to the stigma of a plant of the same species. Fertilisation is the fusion of male nuclei with nuclei (egg cell nucleus and endosperm nucleus) within the embryo sac.

6 The life cycle of mammals is diploid, only the gametes are haploid. The life cycle of flowering plants has a gametophyte (haploid) phase and a sporophyte (diploid) phase.

7 Meiosis produces haploid cells from diploid cells, permitting fertilisation to follow. Also it contributes to genetic variability by permitting random assortment of maternal and paternal homologous chromosomes, and recombinations of segments of individual maternal and paternal homologous chromosomes.

8 Once an organism with a commercially advantageous genome has been produced (e.g. by artificial selection or genetic modification), cloning yields a large number of identical copies, e.g. for sale.

9 A plasmid is a small circular length of DNA that is independent of the chromosome, and commonly found in the cytoplasm of many (but not all) species of bacteria.

Chapter 5

1 Only about 10% of the food matter fed to livestock adds to the body mass of the animals, and therefore is potentially available to humans who later feed on the livestock. On the other hand, grain fed directly to humans is fully available.

2 See 'Legumes of forage crops and pastures', page 61.

3 **a)** About day 40 after emergence of the seedling (see graph).
   b) Nitrates are reduced to ammonium ions (in the root cells). The ammonium ions are then combined with an organic acid, forming glutamic acid (an amino acid). Other amino acids are formed from this amino acid by transamination (switching of amino group to other organic acids). Then proteins are formed from a linear sequence of particular amino acids, condensed together by peptide bonds (at ribosomes, in cells where protein synthesis is required).
   c) Translocated in the phloem.
   d) See 'The carbon pathway of photosynthesis', page 33.
   e) Proteins are broken down (enzymatically) to their constituent amino acids and these are transported in the phloem to the developing seeds and fruits (grains).

4 See 'Photosynthesis in C_4 plants' and Figure 5.14, page 55.

5 Ability to survive in periods of extreme drought, and natural resistance to the local pests that threaten survival of less adapted plants.

6 See Figure 5.21 (page 58) and page 60

7 A more-or-less unlimited supply of sugar from the host plant in which it is 'housed' in root nodules. Sugar is respired to release energy for the fixation of nitrogen.

8 High levels of salts (ions) in soil slows/prevents water uptake by the root hairs of most plants, and therefore leads to death of the natural flora. Without plants growing in soil, wind blows away the topsoil, leaving mostly the heavier, sand particles.

Chapter 6

1 Growth is the more-or-less irreversible increase in size and amount of dry matter. Development is the change in the degree of complexity that accompanies growth.

2 See Figure 4.22, page 46.

3 In cells just inside the seed coat called the aleurone layer.

4 Midway through interphase (the longest stage in the cell cycle), during cell growth.

5 The quantities of IAA are so low, it is the bioassay that is sensitive to the tiny but significant differences in amount that occur.

6 Solar tracking keeps the photosynthetic leaves orientated to receive maximum illumination.

7 Large proteins in which non-protein material is attached, e.g. chlorophyll, haemoglobin.

8 Light:
   • is required for the manufacture of sugar by photosynthesis and for photosynthetic phosphorylation (generation of ATP using light energy) (pages 3 and 32)
   • inhibits extension growth in length of herbaceous stems (page 64)
   • results in positive phototropic responses in stems, leaves (and flowers) – solar tracking (page 72)
   • promotes expansion of leaf blades (page 64)
   • is required for the synthesis of chlorophyll (page 64)
   • triggers the switch from vegetative growth to flowering in many plants, depending upon the length of the light and dark periods within the 24 hour cycle of day and night (page 74)
   • is required to trigger germination in some seeds (page 66).

Chapter 7

1 In high salt environments water uptake by roots may be slowed (why?), so the slowing of transpiration would be advantageous.

2 Washed away into the ground water, or carried away in streams and rivers (leading to eutrophication of natural waters).

Chapter 8

1 See Figure 2.11 (page 9) and Figures 2.13 and 2.14 (pages 10–11).

2 Cork cells and secondary phloem.

Glossary

abscission   the shedding of leaves (and other organs); an abscission layer forms at the leaf stalk base

androecium   the male part of flowers, the stamens

annual plants   complete their life cycle from seed germination to seed production and death in one season

annual ring   annual increment of secondary xylem consisting of early and late wood

autotrophic   an organism that can generate its own food supply from organic and inorganic compounds (e.g. green plants)

bark   the tissue external to the vascular cambium in woody stems and roots

bud   stem apex covered by developing leaves – an embryonic shoot

calyx   the ring of sepals to the outside of the flower

cambium   a lateral meristem, e.g. a layer of cells between xylem and phloem in the vascular bundles; later cambium may develop between the bundles

capitulum   a type of inflorescence in which a large number of florets are all borne on the same level on the enlarged and flattened summit of the peduncle (flower stalk)

cellulose   polysaccharide of many glucose units, major constituent of cell walls, fibrous structure

chloroplast   organelle of green cells, containing chlorophyll; site of photosynthesis

coleoptile   sheath surrounding the apical meristem and developing leaves of the grass embryo

collenchyma   supporting tissue to young organs, living cells, walls thickened unevenly with cellulose

cork   protective tissue of dead, impermeable cells formed by the cork cambium in woody stems and roots

corolla   ring of petals on the flower

cotyledon   the first leaf of the embryo

cuticle   a thin layer of fatty substance on the outer wall of epidermal cells

cytoplasm   the part of the protoplasm that is not the nucleus; transparent, viscous liquid containing membranes and organelles

dicotyledons   plants having two seed leaves in the embryo, usually with net-veined leaves

diploid   double the chromosome number of the gamete; number of chromosomes present in all the vegetative cells

endodermis   surrounds the stele in the root; cells contain the casparian strip in their radial walls

epidermis   outermost layer of cells, one cell thick, around leaves and stem, often with stomata

fibre   an elongated, lignified cell with tapered ends

gametophyte   the plant generation that produces gametes

growth   results in an irreversible increase in size and amount of protoplasm

guard cells   a pair of specialized epidermal cells which, with the aperture between them, form a stoma

gynoecium   all the carpels (the female part of the flower) of a single flower

herbaceous   plants that have no persistent parts above ground, and are not woody

hormones   growth-regulating substances produced in minute amounts, often bringing about effects in another part of the plant

inflorescence   a flowering branch above the last stem leaves, including bracts and flowers

ion uptake   an active process carried out in the roots, selective

medullary rays   radial strands of parenchyma cells in xylem and phloem

meristem   a tissue that produces cells that undergo differentiation to form mature tissues

meiosis   a process of cellular division during which the chromosome number in the cells produced is half that in the diploid cell

mesophyll   the photosynthetic, parenchymatous tissue of leaves

monocotyledons   plants having one cotyledon in the embryo, leaves parallel-veined

mitosis   ordinary nuclear division in which the chromosomes are duplicated

node   the point on the stem where leaves are attached

parenchyma   living, thin-walled cells; makes up the bulk of the plant

pericycle   part of the ground tissue of the stele between the vascular tissue and the endodermis

phloem   the vascular tissue responsible for transport of organic materials in the plant

plumule   shoot apex of the embryo

procambial strand   a primary meristem that undergoes differentiation to form primary vascular tissue

receptacle   the expanded end of a flower stalk bearing flower parts

root hair   an extension of an epidermal cell of the root that grows between soil particles and aids absorption of water and ions

secondary thickening   formation of additional, secondary vascular tissue by activity of cambium, with an accompanying increase in diameter of stem or root

sporophyte   the plant generation that produces spores from which the gametophyte generation develops

stele   core of vascular tissue in the centre of root or stem

stomata   pores in the epidermis of plants

suberin   complex fat material in cell walls (e.g. cork), hence 'suberised'

translocation   movement of organic material in the plant, mostly in the phloem

transpiration   loss of water vapour from the aerial parts of land plants

vacuole   cavity in the cytoplasm containing an aqueous solution

vascular bundle   a strand of conducting tissue

xerophyte   a plant adapted to dry habitats

xylem vessels   the vascular tissue mainly responsible for the conduction of water and mineral salts throughout the plant; also provides mechanical support

Index